Football Crazy

With *photographs* by
Stephen Leighton

First pubiished in 1995 by New Words, Bristol.
© The contributors
© Photographs, Stephen Leighton
ISBN 1 872971 54 7

'Football Crazy' is published as a partnership
between National Westminster Life Assurance
Ltd, South West Arts, Redcliffe Press Ltd.,
Avon Library Service and the Literature
Development Consultant for Bristol and Avon.

♻ National Westminster Life Assurance

● ●

British Cataloguing-in-Publication Data.
A catalogue record for this book is available
from the British Library.

Design by (01372 722275) barefoot

Printed by Longdunn Press Ltd, Bristol.

LINE UP

Illustration by Richard Loveridge

Foreword

Football Crazy has been produced in partnership between NatWest Life Assurance, South West Arts, Avon Library Service, Redcliffe Press and the Literature Development Consultant for Bristol and Avon.

It is the third book in the 'New Words' series, which was set up to publish books for and by the people of Bristol and Avon. The theme of 'football memories' for this latest book is one which has universal appeal - for people of all ages and all sections of the community. We have fond memories of football - be they good or otherwise - particularly when we in Bristol have such a strong footballing tradition!

NatWest Life Assurance is delighted to be associated with this publication, particularly as it brings all of us under a common banner, not only of football, but also of literature and the sharing of human experience.

I hope you enjoy the many, varied contributions in this book.

Lawrence Churchill
Managing Director
NatWest Life and Investment Services.

Illustration by Lucy Johnson

Introduction - Kick Off

David Foot

Someone came up, long ago, with 'working class theatre'. There aren't many better descriptions of our national game. Forget, for a moment, those prosperous-looking wing collared elders who sat round the oak tables and helped to launch the game. Or forget the luvvies and the intellectual trendies who make a great point of being seen at the premiership these days.

Don't be fooled by the grandiose corporate hospitality aspects: with waiters outnumbering the ball-boys, and sponsors appearing to have more say than the managers during the normally garrulous dressing room exchanges at the interval. These are necessary metaphors of the present game. But they don't encapsulate the true emotions of professional football.

Much more accurately, the Saturday afternoon match is a kind of theatre of the people. The plot is uncertain but carries a dozen different options. The audience can applaud the hero and hoot the villain; if they don't think much of the hammy old actor-manager, they can vocally let him know. In the best traditions of drama, they can laugh out loud at the comic lines. They can roar with delight one moment - or weep the next.

Out on the field, there are the bit players, the faithful journeymen (running over every blade of grass) and the principals who have the best parts and pick up most of the headlines.

Just as the dew-eyed groupies queue up at the stage door for a glimpse and maybe an autograph from a handsome leading actor, so the soccer fans stand in the rain - for a snatched word or signature - in the car park at the end of the match.

For many, football fills the emotional void, offering its own aura of glamour. It's tribal and exciting. Out in front, the players in their shimmering shirts bring colour and movement to the social scene.

Until I was a teenager the only games I saw were on the village green. My team played in light blue and dark blue. I knew them all and I cheered my head off. I only wanted them to win, seldom analysing how well individually they played. In truth, I was probably blind to their faults. During the week they worked at the twine factory, the saw mills and the kitchen gardens at the big house; on Saturday, they were pulling on those blue shirts and searching for a communal victory. I shared that hope.

My early heroes were timeless names like Pongo Waring and Sam Hardy, Billy Meredith (with his legendary toothpick) and Arthur Grimsdell, Steve Bloomer and the corner flag-sized Hughie Gallacher. I had no idea which of them came first; I just pretended I'd seen them play. On winter evenings I propped my albums of cigarette cards against the oil lamp to read and learn by heart the captions of each footballer.

How I loved the colours of Norwich and Motherwell then. How I loved those austere hair styles, partings in the middle. As a six year old I combed my hair precociously in the same way. Nowadays the boys try to turn themselves into coiffured clones of Gazza. Over tea on Saturdays I listened with my father to the football results on the wireless. I sat , with pencil poised, to document them; my father sat with eternal optimism, Littlewoods coupon on his lap. Just once he won the four aways - and his reward of just under 10 bob was viewed as a fortune.

From boyhood I was seduced by soccer. It was pure wonderland when a wing half called Joe Payne played centre forward for the first time and scored 10 goals against Bristol Rovers. I was in a barber's shop waiting my turn, when George Mutch netted the Cup Final winner from the penalty spot in the last minute of extra time for Preston North End in 1938. I swear Mr Fox, the barber, cut a customer's cheek with a cut-throat razor in his excitement. As for me, I buried my head in a big white handkerchief and shared the anguish of the Huddersfield skipper who gave away the penalty.

The appeal of the game was never lost. I devoured every inch on the back pages. The result was that I could quote every publicity gimmick dreamed up by Arsenal's urbane George Allison; could proudly give the low down on Major Frank Buckley's use of so-called monkey glands at Wolves; could talk authoritatively at elementary school about Arsenal's record £14,000 fee for Bryan Jones. "He's never going to be as good as Alex James," I said. And so it proved, though the war cruelly curtailed the little Welshman's career.

After the war, the nation's *Green Uns* and *Pink Uns* became for me required reading and the epitome of current literature.
I doted on Raich Carter and Peter Doherty, on Tom Finney, the plumber and Wilf Mannion, the artist. I marvelled at the cockiness of Len Shackleton and was still ecstatic when he got his come-uppance against Yeovil in that historic cup-tie.
I saw no shame in idolatry. Eddie Hapgood and Vic Woodley were two of my heroes and I was thrilled to meet them when they came later to play Bath City. My head was in an even greater whirl when, through a quirk of good fortune, I found myself playing in the same cricket team as Ted Drake and Alec Stock.

Drake was a battering ram of an uncomplicated centre forward, all heart and courage. Stock was the handsome young army officer, son of a Somerset miner, with whom I used to pull up the corner flags and help collect the tea cups in the minuscule dressing room at Huish after a home game.

Managers always interested me. There were Stan Cullis, John Harris and John Carey who never swore. There were those who could somehow cram half a dozen expletives into every sentence. Most of them were bad at appraising a match. You came to realise they saw only one side. In fact, as fans we're all probably guilty of that. Bill Shankly, a notoriously bad loser, stormed out of Ashton Gate on one occasion when City had more than held Liverpool. "We routed you," he said. And he believed it.

My sentimental view of professional football is much influenced by nostalgia. In spirit, I'm still standing on some rickety terrace, pram wheels sticking through, with steaming Bovril in my hand. Still walking to the Valley, past Sam Bartram's shop. Still at Highbury, screaming to Arthur Milton to sprint past his full back as if he were going for a sharp single at the County Ground. Still buying *Charles Buchan's Monthly*, or being shown some of his 26 caps by Billy Wedlock.

The uglier elements of crowd behaviour have gone perilously close to turning me away from football forever. So have some of the stereotyped coaching, declining characters, avaricious agents, ruthless marketing and the impersonal elements of more recent years. What must never be lost is the bond between player and fan.

Could anything have been more perfect than the way, back in the 1950s, Bristol Rovers were known to stop the team coach in Muller Road before a cup-tie, so that the players could walk the last few hundred yards with the supporters? I remember former City managers who would occasionally forsake the touchline and stand with the fans for the 90 minutes. Romantic (and canny) stuff.

The memories are imperishable. They are historic, heroic and certainly at times - as this book implies - crazy. Go on to turn the pages and you'll know what I mean.

Illustration by Rachel Grigg

9

Must be Crazy

Martin Powell

Some people seem to regard football supporting as an exercise in statistics - they remember every date, scoreline and goal average with loving reverence.

For me it is a much more abstract affair - great games stick in the mind, fantastic goals get better and better as you relive them time and again - but the years of cheering on the players in red at Ashton Gate all merge into one tense, but glorious blur of colour, spectacle and passion.

I couldn't tell you if it was the 30th minute or the 48th minute - or even who our opponents were - but I remember Norman Hunter taking a long time to tie his bootlace before he swung over a free-kick that ended in a vital goal. And I remember he grinned and winked at us lads in the Enclosure before he swung that trusty left foot. And I remember Keith Fear tricking a goalkeeper at the Covered End by standing behind him and dashing in to take the ball away from him as he went to roll it out to his full-back and his dance of delight afterwards. Is that really why all goalkeepers now routinely check over their left shoulder before they distribute the ball?

Ernie Hunt with his fashionable droopy moustache and middle-aged spread worked his magic at free-kicks with a modified version of his famous "Match of the Day" kick where the ball was flicked up by one player to be volleyed by another. After the television exposure, those at the top in football thought it was too entertaining and outlawed it on the basis that the ball was touched twice. Once at Ashton Gate Ernie introduced us all to a version where one player stood with his legs apart and Ernie flicked it up to be volleyed with one foot. It never seemed terribly successful but the anticipation as they lined up for the kick was worth the admission price on its own.

Some days are logged firmly on the calendar for all supporters - knocking the mighty Leeds United team out of the FA Cup at Elland Road after a 1-1 draw at Ashton Gate was a day no City fan will forget. But although the statisticians can tell you the names of all the players and the timing of the goal from Donny Gillies it is events outside the ground that are etched on my mind.

The long ponderous train journey to a strange northern land where the only grass seemed to be inside the superb stadium. The ride on a packed double-decker bus to the ground looking out on vast areas of rubble and half demolished streets. Then, after the game, seeing a grown man cry - a Leeds United fan so confident of his team's ability that he had booked his holiday around a trip to Wembley to see them in the Cup Final. Through his tears he congratulated us on a great fighting team.

Others took it more badly. As we passed a red and white sign above a car showroom saying Bristol Street Motors a number of Leeds United fans gathered to throw stones at it - and later at our train as we passed under a bridge, starting the unbelievably joyous journey south.

I don't know how long before the end Donny Gillies scored but it seemed an awful long time as we whistled maniacally for the referee to finish the match. He awarded a free kick to Leeds on the edge of the box and as you looked at Peter Lorimer lining up it seemed there was no way we would survive - but we did.

Supporting Bristol City - a team whose only FA Cup Final appearance was so long ago you would have to be a centenarian to remember it - is all about being part of the crowd and having fun with the other fans. In defeat - and we have seen many - there is also humour. Losing 5-0 at home to Fulham one week the Covered End sang in unison "We're so shit it's unbelievable". The chants were a great part of the fun when we were younger.

"If I had the wings of a sparrow, If I had the wings of a crow (Chris Crowe) I'd fly over Eastville tomorrow and shit on the bastards below" was one of my favourites in the 1960s, along with "Send Bert Tann to Vietnam" to the tune of Michael Rowed The Boat Ashore.

Some players seem to have an affinity with the fans. Others seem to misunderstand what we are all doing behind the goal every game - they think we are there to blindly cheer them on, while we know we are there to criticise and goad them into better performances.

Those who have won the affection of the Ashton Gate crowd over the years include Mike Gibson - our greatest ever goalkeeper. "Gibbo" delighted us with his ritual at the beginning of each game - taking three steps and touching the crossbar to wild cheers - it didn't really matter if he let in seven after that - he had done his bit to entertain us.

In more modern times "Jacki" Dziekanowski with his impish grin and outrageous skills may not have been regarded as much of an asset by some of his team-mates but he had the charisma to keep the fans laughing and talking - far more than any of the "sensible" footballing heads around him. He will live long in the memory for that.

The penalty-missing exploits of Gordon Owen - in successive games his misses cost promotion and a second cup win at Wembley - will always be recorded by the statisticians. But will they record the fact that when he moved from Ashton Gate it was reported in the *Evening Post* that his wife was homesick for the north and did not want him playing at Ashton Gate? Or that when he first returned to Ashton Gate as an opponent on his first run towards the Covered End the fans rose as one, singing "Gordon Owen - does your wife know you're here?"

How can statistics truly sum up the feelings of that first trip to Wembley in the bizarrely-named Freight Rover Trophy. On paper it seems a dull event. In reality it was a lifetime highlight. The motorway trip a tear-jerking blur of red and white scarves flying from car, van and coach windows. Glyn Riley sliding straight-legged towards the crowd and getting a touch of cramp. The Wembley scoreboard reading 3-0. "Gibbo" getting his own special ovation as he came on to the pitch. Singing 3-0 for three solid hours until voices were hoarse and I swear I heard Wembley echo to the sound of "We've won the van, we've won the van, ee aye addio, we've won the van."

But the most memorable moment was simply standing on the terraces at Wembley and seeing all those familiar faces from Ashton Gate in such unfamiliar surroundings and launching into "Drink Up Thee Zyder" - a song never heard at Wembley before.

Glory days indeed. And there are other moments just as sweet. I still have a vivid picture of streams of smiling City fans coming down a set of steps at Eastville. I was looking back trying to persuade my mate Alan Holbrow to come down off a crash barrier where he stood red scarf aloft, face contorted in ecstasy shouting "4-1" over and over again - for we had beaten those strange men from Bath (who then played in their traditional plain blue shirts and not the clown outfits they now insist on) on their own ground by a great score.

It had all seemed so different at half-time as we had gone in 1-0 down - but the Gas hadn't reckoned on the skills of Keith Fear or the 40 mph wind which was blowing towards the Tote End.

We once made it into the First Division - who can forget the crowds gathering around the edge of the pitch ready to lift Clive Whitehead, "Sir" Geoffrey Merrick and the rest shoulder high in celebration?

Months later the streets around Ashton Gate were filled with anticipation as we prepared to set off for Highbury and a First Division game against Arsenal. How many other fans saw Paul Cheeseley almost miss the bus? He was late, leaving his bacon sandwich in the Robins Café and all the other players were on board and the coach tooting its horn - as Cheeseley ran to get on, the bus kept moving further and further away - teasing him. As they went off into the distance my mate Neil Barnes said: "How can that bunch of jokers ever expect to play against Arsenal?" - hours later we saw Cheeseley soar above the Arsenal defence to give us a 1-0 away win.

Years of tedium and journeymen players are endured for those moments. It is the comments of the crowd around you that keep you going. We have been moved out of the East End into the Carling Atyeo stand and we have lovely facilities these days. But the comments of the crowd remain as fresh as ever. A chap called Dave Collins always seems to find a seat by me. During one dour relegation battle he asked: "Has anyone brought a pack of cards" and as the crowd slumped below 3,000 for one pointless, featureless match he suggested a Mexican Wave!

Managers, players, terraces, chairmen - they all come and go. We fans are there every week. Statistically it makes no sense - but it's what football is all about.

Get your Knits Out for the Lads

Joyce Woolridge

I'd like to tell the story of how I began to love football as a small girl in Manchester, long before I'd ever seen my first match, but I don't know how to begin. I'll have to find some way of conveying to readers how exciting, but also how very dissimilar, a girl's apprenticeship as a fan of the great game is to the familiar stories told by boys who have grown up to become, well, bigger boys on the terraces. I've read them all. The nostalgia for the Pannini sticker album with the missing players, the Esso World Cup Coin Collection similarly yet tantalisingly almost complete. "I was a mascot," even "I was a hooligan." Unfortunately, or rather fortunately, I wasn't either of those two, and my collecting instincts were limited to World Cup Willie Badges which you got free with a particularly corrosive brand of two-tone nougat. Though to call it a collection is cheating; they were all the same. Unlike the hamster males I haven't preserved these lovingly, my legacy being limited to a dental disaster zone that can pick up Russian radio on clear nights. As we are often told, it's different for girls.

Don't misunderstand me, I'm as obsessed by football as any man I know. After growing up in Stretford in the heartlands of United mania, passing a wall with "Man U the religoin" (poor spelling but great theology) daubed on it every day on my way to school, it was my destiny.

Like other girls, I'm sure, I showed my devotion and nurtured my love for the only United in an uniquely female way - by knitting and colouring. Now, honestly, will my autobiography of a life told through football, wittily titled "Knits Out For The Lads" have a hope of ever reaching out to the mass audience with chapter headings like "Casting On My Scarf As The Reds Go For Euro Glory", "The Wool Runs Out" (cleverly coded reference here to Man City's robbery of the League Title from United by one point in 1968) and "I start another exercise book of match reports and pictures"?

Bear with me as I reveal some of the significant moments in this contribution to women's writing which will probably receive the recognition it deserves only long after my demise. In a more enlightened age it will top the bestseller list when every team has its women players and I have spent a glorious ten years as England manager. (Women's fantasies about football are not, you see, about scoring with players, but scoring in important matches. However, as no amount of trundling round the Downs being jeered at by fit youths playing Saturday soccer will ever make me the new George Best I have opted for a top managerial role.)

To set the scene for the two chapters I am about to preview, before the first I have just spent two years knitting a ten foot long red and white scarf which is extremely heavy, very hot and very itchy. Around the production of this I have woven the end of Sir Matt Busby's managership, Bestie on the booze, the joy of my first visit to Old Trafford, and other sagas. Then, recalling how this item of high fashion became an enormous liability, throttling me, tripping me up, tripling its weight when wet and, ultimately, exposing me to ridicule when printed "silk" scarves replaced the Doctor Who look, I move forward to the day I finally lost it, along with some of my innocence about the game.

"Chapter 10: I lose something I will never get back ..."

It's not over dramatic to say that the last time that ten foot red and white snake entwined itself around my legs, nearly landing me flat on my face, might have meant that I never actually saw United win the League Championship again. In 1975 my brother took me to White Hart Lane to see Docherty's flying wingers beat Spurs. It was a very ugly match. Not on the pitch, where the football was free flowing and fast and there were some wonderful goals. The real action, for many, was elsewhere. My away game experience was decidedly limited. Football violence, then approaching its peak, was something I'd only ever seen on TV. My initiation wasn't long in coming.

The segregation of fans had been intelligently done. We were in the bottom of a two tier stand; the home fans were in the top. Every one of them seemed to have a can. The world's longest scarf gave them a highly recognisable target. Colours alone wouldn't have started the hail of missiles, but we were standing next to the terrace companion from hell. Sensing a potentially explosive situation developing, he responded in an appropriate manner by turning to the opposition supporters above us, forming a circle with his thumb and forefinger, and making a gesture, the significance of which I pretended to know but didn't. The sky darkened as the tins rained down. I suddenly understood the gesture; it meant we had to get away from the idiot next to us.

Five minutes before the end, my brother - alarmed by the outbreaks of fighting - decided we ought to leave early. As we emerged from the away fans' exit, we saw why that wasn't a good idea. Spurs fans were charging towards us. We stood, alone in the road, one of us unmistakably identified as the enemy. "Get rid of that!" hissed our kid. I did what he said, my fingers trembling, but the heirloom wasn't going to go without a struggle. It tripped me up, and I raised my head to see an army of bovver boots advancing and my life poetically flashing in front of me. Just as it looked hopeless, a policeman riding a white horse suddenly appeared. He made his mount rear up and the mob retreated at the sight of its flailing hooves. I was frozen until he bellowed, "P**s off, out of it, quick!" We p**sed off out of it, very quickly, as directed. Only the scarf received a good kicking.

I don't remember how we boarded the bus to safety but I can't forget what I saw as it tried to move down a road blocked by the mass fight going on all around the ground. Fight is the wrong word. It makes it all sound too honourable, rather Marquis of Queensberry. The aim was to isolate someone so that fifteen heroes could boot him in the head. I tried not to look and felt sick to my stomach. Many of those with me on the top deck cheered and commented gleefully on the appalling sight below. I really did lose something that I had spent my childhood making that day.

"Chapter 20: Every Picture Tells A Story ..."

I'm sitting in my parents' home in Manchester with my little nephew Sam, playing drawing and colouring in footballers. He, like myself at that age, has never seen a football match, but he has been completely indoctrinated about Manchester United by his adoring adults. He loves this particular drawing game, but not as much as I do. From the age of ten onwards, I made up football scrapbooks, full of match reports adapted from the *Manchester Evening News* and my own renditions of their action photographs of players. As Sam leans over me, grunting softly with the fierce concentration of the small child, doing the pitch with sweeping jagged strokes of his felt tip, I see myself many years before, carefully applying a lurid carmine red to a shirt from my giant paintbox. A sigh of satisfaction escapes me as I finish and add the caption "Young Brian Kidd had an outstanding game". It really did look like Brian Kidd.

This was the first of a small library of these home-produced books. One day my uncle Bob came to visit, picked one up, and, unaware of my sources, was mightily impressed by the quality of my junior prose. The last report was a stirring account of a semi-final replay between Man U and Don Revie's Leeds. I was putting the finishing touches to a masterly painting of the Charlton brothers, Bobby and Jackie, tussling for the ball.

"That's a good drawing, love." His compliment made me very proud. "But doesn't Brian Kidd have a lot more hair than that?"

Despite endless practice, I never could draw anyone but Brian Kidd, and relied upon the caption to identify the particular player. But through that drawing and writing I came to believe that I had been there at those matches, part of the excitement.

Sam has already chosen who we are drawing. Though Sam's replica shirt says "No 11, Giggs", he has solemnly declared that we are drawing Eric. The temperamental French genius soon takes shape, and, as he does, I notice that time has served only to improve my technique. Sam's Dad, home from work, is greeted by his son running towards him waving the joint production. Dad is impressed.

"That's really good, our Joyce," he exclaims, genuinely surprised by my artistry. "But Brian Kidd's nose is never that big."

I won't be winning any awards for my book if it is ever written, but what I've shown you may serve to remind people that there are other types of football stories. These provide a gentler space where dreams can be woven and loyalties forged.

Match of the Day

Anthea Youens

It's Saturday night - shall we go out for a drink luv'?
No sweetheart, I'm watching Match of the Day.
Oh no! not again -
that's what you always say!

Have I told you how wonderful you look tonight?

How about a bottle of wine, soak in the bath and an early night?
eh, eh!
Surely even that sounds better than Match of the Day?

Sorry Bob -
You've done your best to lead my astray,
but even Ryan Giggs couldn't stop me watching Match of the Day!
- or could he?

Fertility Festival or Lesson in Love?

Liz Loxley

"It's a fertility festival. Eleven sperms trying to get into the egg." - Björk, popstar, quoted in *The Independent on Sunday Review* May 28 1995.

"Football isn't Britain's favourite sport." - Triumph bra advertisement.

Sunday morning, 10.50 am: a time more fittingly spent in bed listening to the Archers omnibus but I'm sitting on a specially chartered train on my way to Wembley to see Bristol Rovers in the 1995 second division play-off finals. Sitting reading the Sunday papers where the dearth of pre-match coverage is cancelled out by the above quotes from the *Independent on Sunday Review*. Football 1 - Sex 1. We're travelling to Wembley on a promise and the mood is enhanced by club stewards handing out deflated green balloons like condoms on an 18-30 jolly. It may be like some sort of pre-coital ritual but it's innocent fun; safe sex, safe football with families travelling together, children with blue and white quartered painted faces, men with green and black Afro wigs and a generous smattering of well filled specially designed T shirts to mark the event. And the train, dating from the 1950s, harks back to a more innocent era, the days before free love and football hooliganism. To days when planet football spun in a different orbit and when a perm was something connected with the football pools and not perched on top of the head of every one-time aspiring England footballer.

It's a stately ride to the country's capital city and greatest ground; rattling past the green fields of Oxfordshire, the blue wrinkled rivers Avon and Isis and, finally, the Thames. A guard at Reading enters into the footballing spirit, sporting a Reading FC hat. From Reading, the journey seems longer than Rovers' trek to Wembley. Finally, past one o'clock, the train pulls in at Wembley Central and we pile out, jostling like eager teenagers on an away day, clutching our balloons (some now inflated).

The walk to Wembley is punctuated by a visit to a vast, cavernous bar packed to the rafters already with Rovers fans and over the odd pint or two the passion swells and we start to sing, full of hope and glory: "Goodnight Irene, I'll see you in my dreams". "We love you Rovers, we do". Then, with beer in our bellies and hope in our hearts, we start the second leg of our journey.

My memories of the match itself are snapshots, pinpricks of pleasure and pain. What I remember first is the feeling of pride when the team walk out on to the pitch to the Gashead roar. I'm like a parent at school sports day, thinking how smart the players look in their green and black quartered kit, anxiously checking how nervous they look with a lump like a football in my own throat and my hands becoming slimy with sweat. They play like nervous men in the first half with Huddersfield, muscular and powerful in the air, dominating the game for periods of time.

There are still chances for Rovers but there are a clutch of corners for Huddersfield. David Pritchard clears off the line, Andy Gurney clips the ball on to his own bar. Then the Huddersfield goal; a triple whammy of headers finally guided into the net by their top scorer, Andy Booth. There is scarcely time to consider the calamity of this unwelcome blow when Marcus Stewart swivels in the box at the far end of the pitch and poaches the equaliser. Football crazy is a phrase best saved for moments like this: a distilled moment of ecstasy when adrenalin bursts through the body obliterating everything else.

Second half, Rovers play like we always knew they could. Channing strikes, it looks for a moment as if it is going in, but it flies wide. The ball rebounds from the bar from Stewart's header and Taylor shoots off target. At the other end, Parkin, back pedalling, makes a superb save. At our end, Stewart cuts in but shoots wide. Substitution: Browning for Taylor; Dunn for Crosby and 2-1 replaces 1-1 on the scoreboard as Billy scores for Huddersfield. Rovers don't give up: Browning shoots and the goalkeeper saves well; Stewart again sees one of his efforts come off the bar and Browning misses from the rebound. However, it proves to be in vain.

It all ends in tears. On the pitch, my man of the match, Marcus Stewart, seems inconsolable. I realise that, despite my own bitter disappointment, I want to help lift the team's spirits and that desire catches fire among the Gasheads. When the team don their blue and white quarters and come to acknowledge the fans, giant choruses of "Goodnight Irene" ring out once more. So we lost the match, but far from this being a game full of sound and fury, signifying nothing, I realise that, in a season that could have ended up in mid-table mediocrity, the team achieved something by making it to Wembley. We've had a great day out and love is not too strong a word to express the emotion that pours out from the crowd to the players.

So it's back to Bristol. No-one seems to want to talk about the game in detail, the wound is too deep at present. We play cards, doze a little, watch the passing countryside as intensely as a football match. We do not mention the ball hitting the bar in the dying minutes of the game.

On Monday morning, thousands of Bristol Rovers fans line streets of the city to show their appreciation for what the team achieved rather than mourn what they didn't. I'm at Eastville, the spiritual home of the club, dodging parked cars in the Tesco car park to applaud the players on their open top bus. The flags, banners, balloons and T shirts are proudly on display and while there is not the crazy, joyous atmosphere that promotion would have brought, there is still pride, warmth, admiration and gratitude. "Goodnight Irene, we'll see you in our dreams," "We love you Rovers, we do." Football may be a fertility festival but this Bank Holiday morning, with promotion only seen in our dreams, this is our lesson in love.

A Season in the Life of ... A Bristol City Supporter

John Hill

Sometime during a Saturday morning in the middle of August I awake and stumble out of bed with more enthusiasm and as much expectation as a five year old on Christmas morning. Visions of men in red and white have disturbed the night's slumbers but it's Russell Osman, not Santa Claus, that holds the key to this Season's Greetings, and it is a parcel full of goals, a promotion challenge and an away trip to Old Trafford in the Third Round of the F.A. Cup that I want in my stocking.

Choosing what to wear is a problem. I haven't got round to visiting the City Shop to buy this year's team strip and wearing last year's would be a worse couturiel nightmare than turning up in flared jeans and a kipper tie. At last I arrive at Ashton Gate just in time to join in the frenetic discussions in the Supporters' Club. There is no time to exchange pleasantries about balmy days on Majorca or the Greek Islands. Much more pressing is the fact that Tinnion and Martin both have long term injuries, rumour has it that some young players are about to be introduced and who should play in the back four, Harriot or Munro? The headaches of team selections but still the manager could leave it to us if he so wished.

The season kicks off. It is disappointing to drop two points at home to Sunderland but a week and an away win at Bolton convinces me that my bet on City to win the First Division is safe and that the odds of 28 to 1 were a generous act of lunacy on the part of William Hill's. An American friend accompanies me to the Port Vale match. He finds it difficult to understand why it is that it is the Bristol City fans that seem to hurl most abuse at the home team. Even harder is it to convince him that City haven't won, and I give up trying to explain that Junior Bent's goal was offside. Having missed the Notts County game because of work commitments I leave the Middlesbrough match ominously realising that I won't have seen a City goal at Ashton Gate by the end of September. With slightly superstitious tendencies and accepting the entire blame for City's lowly league position I wonder should I stop watching them. I work on October 8th. City score and beat Millwall. Perhaps I should start going to Twerton Park to see if my adverse magic wreaks havoc there!

Then comes the Wolves match. More chaos than the Cumberland Basin ten minutes before kick-off time, as Mark Shail is sent off and they score more goals than I can count. It is a black tie the following morning and barely a week later Russell Osman is made the scapegoat. The stage is set for the Second Coming of Joe Jordan. The ecstatic roar that greets his return brings a lump to the throat and almost removes the roof of the Atyeo stand. Swindon can only stand and watch as Junior runs them ragged. Wayne Allison

scores two and City three; surely it must be straight up the table now.

It isn't. A couple of defeats later and poor Marvin Harriot is irrationally blamed for everything including the Bolton defeat. It is difficult to work out which came first - the referee's whistle to start or their goal. If that was the quickest winning goal of the season, the most bizarre is the result of the muddle between Stuart Munro and Keith Welch that limps over the line in the dying seconds at West Bromwich. The cruellest must be Everton's undeserved F. A. Cup winner. But these are all forgotten as Matt Bryant nearly breaks the net against Barnsley. Like manna from Heaven Robert Fleck arrives. Suddenly City are picking up a few points. Although they are still immobile one place from the bottom, calculators begin to click. Mathematically a play off place is still possible.

Dusk begins to fall on the season and Fleck goes back to Chelsea. There are just too many draws and then bang, bang, bang - Derby, Tranmere and the final killer shot, Stoke City. A team that is going to survive doesn't concede a losing goal in the 89th minute. Their goal causes as much pain as any bullet and even I have to admit it is the end. A couple more meaningless fixtures confirm the expected, and the season is put to rest. I gradually drift off and dream of away trips to Crewe and Stockport and - as optimistic as ever - console myself with the thought that City are bound to have the best stadium in the Second Division.

Falling from Grace in the Eyes of a Child

Tony Lewis-Jones

No longer the brash booted hero out of myth
stands the father, faced down by
the crowd of youths who won't return
the football. His only son
knows tears are close; self pity
rising to the throat; witnesses
a cloudy day in Spring
the godhead's irreversible defeat.

Wandering home beneath a shrinking sky
they dare not speak the knowledge they have shared.

Own Goal

Mike Akers

"Oi! Ref! You need glasses!"

A large tattooed away fan was leaning at a dangerous angle over the advertising boards behind the goal to give me the benefit of his wisdom. I had awarded a free kick just outside the penalty area after a badly timed lunge by the away side's full back.

Then I get the old 'eyesight' jibe. Firstly, let me make it clear that I do not need glasses. I have the Specsavers eye test receipts to prove it. I had, however, been instructed by my doctor to take things easy, after a recent bout of stress-related illness. The fan's predictable taunt had set off the little tremor in my left eyelid which is a sure sign I am over-doing it. Resisting the urge to run to the terraces with the glad tidings of my perfect vision, I closed my eyes and began my deep breathing exercises. There was some confusion at this pause in the action. The crowd became restless, the players stood with hands on hips and puzzled expressions on faces. Malcolm, the fourth official - a man I have never really trusted - trotted smugly on to the pitch expecting to take charge. My Karmic balance was restored and, again in harmony with the Universe, I dismissed Malcolm from the field.

The whistle blew, play resumed and the free kick swung into the six yard area. The centre forward rose cleanly above the defence, but his contact was weak and the ball ballooned high and wide. Another wonderful chance had been squandered. The home side had not registered a goal for the last seven weeks. They were a shoddy, hopeless mixture of teenagers on Youth Training Schemes and sad old professionals whose glory days were a decade or more behind them. I felt a strange empathy for this rag bag collection of has been's and never would be's. I awarded them a corner. I felt a twinge of guilt, but hell, they hadn't scored for seven weeks. Their manager had walked out, their ground was about to be demolished and turned into a Do-It-Yourself car park and ride emporium. They were helpless, homeless orphans looking up at me with big sad eyes. It was time life gave them a break.

Of course, the away chaps were not best pleased. Players cursed, saliva bullets ricocheted off the turf, there were a lot of meaningful glares of the "wait till we get down the tunnel" variety. The crowd started, too. There was a large contingent of rabidly partisan away supporters behind the goal. Their team might well be described by commentators as a 'slumbering giant'. Recent signs of an imminent awakening had swelled the travelling hordes. The disputed corner provoked a lusty rendition of an old favourite of mine that sounds a bit like "who's the flanker in the black?" My eye was set off again.

The home side's winger waddled across to the corner flag. Grey haired, pot-bellied, he was a forlornly isolated figure. He stared blankly at the ball as if about to be overwhelmed by the futility of it all. "There is no point," his eyes seemed to tell me. The corner kick soared across the face of the goal. The crowd continued to chant my name and question my sexuality. My eye twitched, my heart leapt and then sank as player after inadequate player failed to master the bobbing, loose ball. The pantomime was ended by a clearance to the edge of the area. To my surprise, I found myself completely unmarked. I controlled the ball with my first touch, then fired a low right footed drive with my second. The keeper made a desperate dive but the ball flew past his despairing hand into the net. I gave a sharp blast on the whistle and signalled to the centre. GOAL!

Pandemonium broke out. I was surrounded by some furious, some curious faces. Fans, players, the press, all were on the pitch. Cameras flashed from every angle. I saw Tom Cruise and Nicole Kidman push their way through the confused mass. Questions and insults mingled with the distant melody of a handful of home fans chanting "One nil, one nil" towards the bemused away end. Gradually I regained control. The melée subsided as I resolutely marched back to the centre circle for the re-start. Both linesmen and Malcolm the weasel waited there, solemnly.

"It is with great regret, following your appalling misconduct that I must relieve you of your duties in this game," said Malcolm without regret. "Please hand over your cards and whistle."

The full enormity of what I had done began to sink in. I was a man of two halves, tears mingled with laughter. I wanted to hug Malcolm and to strangle him all at the same time. He stared at me with steel in his eyes. I did not resist. I handed my tools over to him and began the loneliest walk of them all. There was a strange hush. My head hung low. My career as a referee was over. My career in life assurance would doubtless also take a tumble. Expecting violent damnation, I turned my eyes to heaven in the search for redemption. As I did so I noticed that some people were standing. I looked around the ground. Every man, woman and child was standing to salute my exit. Applause filled my ears. A smile spread across my face and I raised my arms in triumph. I kissed my black jersey and departed the stage forever.

Crazy Boys

Laura Nuttal

Boys are crazy about football. All they ever do at playtime is football, football and more football. Sometimes people fall out in football. They start fighting and they get banned from playing. The girls can still play. That's the problem. Because the girls have got a ball the boys take it off us and that gets me really mad. Sometimes the boys let us play football but we have to stay in the goal. If we let a goal in by mistake we are sent off.

Once a boy in our class hurt his arm and had to have it in a sling but he still played football. Even the football coach was surprised. I think Eric Cantona shouldn't kick people in public and on T.V because that's why the boys start fighting over the ball or whose throw in it is. I wish boys would get fed up with football and play something else.

Chasing the Blues Away

E. J. Gazeley

It isn't our night:
grouse small corps of Pirates
on M4's hard-shoulder, eyeing
tyre puncture, watches quar-
ter-to-eight - Rovers' kick-off
already past. Yet, ever-hopeful
thumbs stick out. Throats choke,
as other fans exhaust.

It isn't our night:

groan Hull defenders, discar-
ding goalie's, ref's lineper-
son's wedlocked birth on seeing
a misdirected punch, red-card,
promotion point, pointedly
pirated away, So, shroud eyes
when tragedy is spotted.

grouch ten Rovers on Hull
City's floodlit pitch, as
player-coach subs untried youth
for only-goalscorer with
relegation fast approaching -
then even more when
knock-out blow lands.

It isn't our night:

Gas-heads vex aboard Hull
bound Rover. Then pirate-
radio station crackles up
winning score with a Goodnight from Irene at four
gobsmacked better-halves,
now absolutely positive -

It isn't!

Illustration by Darren Vickery

In Praise of Mortal Gods

John Murphy

I liked football when I was a kid - although I was under the illusion that the referee stood between the goal posts, and the 'goalkeeper' was the poor sod who put the nets up.

Later, taking a ball to school always guaranteed me a game, as well as bringing me my first real friends. Like my Dad I shouted for the Reds, which was a good enough reason at that age, besides which, our manager was that funny little Scottish fellah who always made it sound so much fun!

But the time I first saw heavenly bodies, and saw my heart truly captured in the name of Liverpool, was on a cold Wednesday night in March 1977: the night Liverpool announced to the world that their long but deserved climb to the top of European football had spectacularly arrived.

The buzz on the streets and around the schoolyards and sitting-rooms of the Red half of the City had slowly built to a crescendo in the aftermath of a weary 1st leg in France, to the extent that by the time 55,043 Red and White sardines - with a few green French ones thrown in for colour - had packed themselves into the Anfield cauldron, the electric atmosphere was so charged that the floodlights were plugged into the stanchions of the stands!

I'd arrived at 5 pm in order to get a good place to stand at the the front of the Kop, only to find that about 10,000 other people had had the same idea: I eventually squeezed my way to the front about ten yards from the right-side corner flag at twenty past seven.

Looking around, my young mind registered the strange sight of thousands of grown men all biting their finger nails in unison. A truly rare phenomenon in those days. Yes, we were nervous.

But the Boot-room Boys had perfected a secret weapon, whose devastating effect was to be likened to the U-boats of WW2 ... enter one David Fairclough!

Super-Sub had already been my hero for some time - we both had red hair - but that night he was to become part of Anfield folklore and crowned a mortal God.

All the team were heroes that night, even now when I think of Keegan two things come to mind; those daft shirts he used to wear with the fly-away collars, and the all important first goal of that night, which not only got the players going, but sent the crowd absolutely crazy. The way 25,000 Koppites surged and swayed should have been very frightening to a young lad like me, yet the only thing which worried me was losing my place - I clung to that lip of concrete on the front wall as if my life depended on it!

When St. Etienne equalised through Bathenay the silence deafened, but it wasn't long before the songs started up again, the air once more filled with that electric excitement. 'Allez les Rouges' was the cry going up around three sides of the ground, drowning out completely the corresponding shouts of the fans down at the 'Anny Road End', then Ray Kennedy gave the Kop its second present of the evening. Now the French were really in trouble.

A man of about 50 picked me up and hugged and kissed me like I was his son, roaring into my ear. "We've won it now, we've won it now!", but the tension was still there. Although we were now 2-1 up and 2-2 on aggregate, we all knew what that away goal meant; we had to score again, and try as we might they seemed to be weathering our attacks. I kept hearing people screaming at the bench, "Try Super-Sub!" "Get that red-headed lad on!", and sure enough the bench raised John Toshack's number with the number 12: Bob Paisley was about to produce his ace-in-the-hole, and what an ace it was!

From the moment Fairclough took to the field the Kop raised their voices even higher, then Kennedy sent the ball from just inside our half, clearing most of their defence for Fairclough to pick up. Some big fellah in their defence seemed to try everything to stop him, but he held on to the ball, getting closer and closer to the goal, the crowd growing louder and louder as he did so. Without stopping, he pulled back the trigger just inside of the area and fired his torpedo - Goooaaal! We all went absolutely crazy! The noise lasted for a full two minutes, everyone singing and dancing and screaming, but there were still a few minutes left and, though still celebrating, we sat out those agonising moments with our hearts in our mouths.

Pheeeep!

That was the signal for the greatest celebrations I'd ever known to begin. Most people didn't even attempt to leave the Kop for a half hour or so, singing our songs of praise to the skies. That night I experienced tears of joy for the first time in my life, real honest-to-goodness tears, and walked home with the coldness of the night replaced by the warmth of the knowledge that I had seen something very special. I didn't care that my Mum didn't know where I'd been, or that I'd be an hour late; no punishment could've diminished the joy I felt. That was the night I saw men become Gods.
Dedicated to Liverpool Supporters Everywhere

Football Calendar

L. Brook

1989

"Yes."

I jumped about a mile. Even from the kitchen I knew United had scored. The cat came flying from the sitting room having been very rudely awakened by his human father's enthusiastic bellow. I shrugged my shoulders to the cat, he blinked back at me.

"One nil," came the latest report on a match which held nil interest for me.

I turned the radio on to a Golden Oldie station in an attempt to drown out further outbursts.

1990

"I've recorded the match. I'll watch it while you're out."

"Good idea. See you later."

When I came back about two hours later he was in the kitchen starting to prepare dinner.

"United won three one. It was a cracker of a game. Pallister played out of his skin."

"Good." I glanced at the cat for his reaction. He blinked back at me.

1991

"D'you mind if I watch the live match this afternoon?"

"No. I'm just going to finish my knitting. It won't bother me."

The cat sat on my lap and went to sleep. I followed my knitting pattern, every now and then having my attention drawn to the match.

"Lin, look at this replay." I gave the replay half a glance and said, "Mm."

"Look at him tugging Bruce's shirt. He's nearly pulled it off his back."

I looked up again, and tutted my disapproval. The cat looked up at me and blinked.

"Ah no. How on earth that didn't go in - it's as if there are garage doors on that goal today. They're doing everything but scoring."

1992

"United are on Match of the Day tonight. Just the highlights. All right if I take a look?" he said casually.

"Yes. I'll have another glass of wine and sit here with you." The cat blinked, and settled down beside me.

"Who's that there? He looks like a dirty player."

"Mark Hughes. He's not dirty, he's tough. Hard to knock off the ball. They all have a go at Hughesy. You watch."

"Oh yes. He is tough. I'd expect him to be writhing around on the ground after that."

"Not Hughes. I bet he's black and blue when he comes off the field. Damn good player. Scores some magnificent goals. You watch."

1992

"Shall we look at Match of the Day tonight?" he asked.

"Are United on?"

"Yes."

"O.K."

The three of us (including the cat) took up our positions for this evening's feast of football. At last they showed the highlights from United's game.

"I like that McClair." I offered. "He looks a bit useful."

"More than a bit. He can score goals too. This is a lovely team, Lin. Play beautiful football. And a couple of seasons ago everyone was criticizing Alex Ferguson. United kept faith with him and it's paying dividends."

"Seems like it."

1993

"I'll record the United match and we can watch it this evening," he said.

"Good idea. I like to hear what the experts say. Alan Hansen's really dishy."

"At least he knows what he's talking about. Not like Brooking."

"Doesn't he?"

"No. He never was any good."

"Oh."

We slumped in front of the television, glasses filled, cat moving from him to me. From time to time an earsplitting yell would rend the air. The cat knew he was safe with me and my knitting.

"My God," I cried. "How on earth did Schmeichel save that?"

"Brilliant. He's made all the difference to the team. I never rated Les Sealey. Look at Schmeichel organising his defence."

He was certainly yelling at them. He was not a pleased man.

"Damn. I've done my pattern wrong watching that. I'll have to sort it out. If anything exciting happens, run the tape back."

"O.K."

1994

"D'you really want to go out tonight?" I asked him.

"Not necessarily. I thought you wanted to."

"I'd sort of like to see Match of the Day."

He beamed at me. "We don't have to go out, of course not. If you'd rather stay in we will."

"Little Ince has really come on, hasn't he?" I said as we watched him hold up the ball and execute a precision pass to Kanchelskis who was racing down the wing.

"Yes, he's really grown up. Now he's stopped answering back he's concentrating on his game."

"D'you know it's no wonder most of this team are internationals," I said, after a fabulous attempt on goal by Giggs. "What skill, what a build up, what patience. What lovely football. They must surely do the double this season."

"No question," he agreed, eyes glued to the silky skills of Cantona. "Look at that."

"Yes," I yelled as the ball hit the back of the net, leaving the goalkeeper well and truly stranded. The cat leapt off my lap.

1995

"Have you asked John to record the United match?" I asked him. "It's on Sky tomorrow."

"I'll do it now," he said, picking up our football video.

Next evening we settled before the screen, my knitting lay in its bag on the floor, the cat in splendid isolation on the settee. No lap was safe in this house any more when United was on T.V.

"Offside," I shouted.

"No Lin," he smiled at me. "Wishful thinking."

"They're not going to catch Blackburn, you know," I said sadly.

"Well, it's not the end of the world," he said,

"and Blackburn are a good footballing side."

"It is the end of the world," I said, "and Blackburn bought its way to the Championship. Anybody can throw money at it."

He smiled again. "But you have to buy the right players and blend them together. Dalgleish has done that. You can't take it away from him."

"And I thought you were a true United fan." I said. "Wash your mouth out." I glanced at the cat. He nodded in agreement.

Three Minutes

Mick Dawle

"And in the corner there, is one of our saddest patients, he spends most of his days just staring into space saying ... Three minutes, just three minutes ... why, why, why?"

"How long has he been doing this?"

"Well most of the time he's been here, which must be nearly 20 years."

"Do you know why?"

"Apparently some years ago there used to be a national football league ... this is going back many years before the Super Premier World League was set up ... and his team was only three minutes away from joining the National Premier League ... he never recovered from the disappointment."

So I'm a Reading supporter. You can't choose your parents, you can't blame your mother for carrying you in her womb while only 400 yards away Elm Park roared to one of the great seasons under manager Ted Drake with Ronnie Blackman scoring 39 goals.

You can't choose where you were born, at times I wished we would move to London or later on Manchester, but it didn't happen.

It often puzzles me what other people do on Saturdays.

I believe it's called the biological clock ... the knowledge that it's 4.40 in England on a Saturday, wherever you are. Whenever it's been 4.40, and for some reason I am shopping and I join the huddle of downcast men around a television shop window where the videprinter is showing the Reading result, it's always a terrible result. That is one of the mysteries of football, the power to manipulate results of games that have already been played. Some seasons you know they will only win if you hear it on the radio, others it's the videprinter while sitting at home with a mug of tea in front of you (of course it has to be the lucky mug). The glorious 1985/86 season promotion was only won through Lou's Dad passing the humbugs round. The act had to be spontaneous otherwise the spell would be broken.

I never found out who Lou was, or his Dad for that matter, but he always seemed to be standing next to us on the terraces. Lou's Dad was there for the last promotion in 1926, it took him 60 years to get the correct ingredients for promotion, and then he probably never knew.

We didn't see him again, and they got relegated two seasons later.

Reading have acquired the tag 'unfashionable Reading'. It shows how little people know. Reading in the 1970s had the first truly ugly player (Percy Freeman) years before Le Tissier and Beardsley made it fashionable to be ugly.

They also had the shortest goal-keeper in Steve Death, the legendary Arthur Wilkie, the only goal-keeper to score two goals in a game, and in 1972 played the only game when there have ever been three players called Dennis Butler on the pitch (2 for Reading and 1 for Doncaster Rovers).

We are proud of our records at Reading.

In the genius of Robin Friday there was a hard drug user playing 20 years before Paul Merson. His life was tragically to end roasted to death on Boxing Day after passing out in a drink-and-drug coma in front of the gas fire.

The football was always secondary, a win seen as a bonus, and an entertaining win, enough to keep you happy all week.

It was often enough just to go and mock your worst player; Reading have generously provided the fans with many over the years. Or taunt the visiting fans on the way to the tea bar with that great song:

"Who ate all the pies? Who ate all the pies? You fat bastard, you fat bastard, who ate all the pies?"

It was best when the fan reacted, showed off his belly and got carted off by the police.

The pleasure used to come from following the same streets to the ground that I had walked along for over 30 seasons; walking across the railway bridge that now comes up to my waist, but remembering when my dad used to lift me up to watch the steam train going underneath.

From parking in the pub car park, the same pub I used to go to with my first girl friend. From walking through the fallen leaves and remembering collecting conkers with my cousins.

However often you thought of giving up going you realised you never could. It was like visiting a sick relative, you felt guilty if you didn't go.

That was enough, until it all got spoilt by the creation of a great foot-balling side. The football began to be important, the desire to win, getting into the play offs, dreaming of the Premier League, knowing this was a once-in-a-lifetime opportunity.

Into the final at Wembley, playing brilliantly, being 2-0 up with a penalty for a 3 goal lead, and still 2-1 up with just three minutes to go.

Say goodbye to Vale Park and the Goldstone Ground, Old Trafford and White Hart Lane beckon ...

'and McAteer's storming through the midfield, a perfect pass to de Freitas, he's past Wdowzcyk ... it's 2-2.

...with three minutes to go Reading have thrown away what seemed to be an impregnable lead, and the state they are in Bolton have to be the winners in extra time.'

"...Three minutes, just three minutes ... why, why, why?"

Spot the Ball

Helen Buckingham

Last night I dreamt
I was watching the football,
only it wasn't a football,
it was a leopard, rotating
adrift between kicks,
like some fifties' motif
on a Liberty pitch.
I gritted my teeth

for I gleaned a low hiss
through the roar of the crowd,
and the fur on my neck
warned that any time now
the design might unravel ...

This morning, over breakfast,
your Game Plan was silence.
(Turned out the Spurs had lost.)

By lunchtime
I'd earnt my spots.

Joe, Nicky and Me

Kathryn Britton

Most of my female - and indeed some of my male friends - find it difficult to understand exactly why football is so important to me. There's probably some dark psychological reason why I prefer to spend Saturday afternoons at Ashton Gate (after watching 'Football Focus' of course), rather than shopping or doing anything constructive. Friends at University, too, were bemused by the fact that I would spend much needed funds on an overnight trip on a Tuesday or Wednesday afternoon, to watch a match that evening and return in time for lectures next day.

Unfortunately the obsession is not only with Bristol City. I am constantly told off for letting my eyes drift to the football screen in the pub. I have been to see Charlton Athletic (my local team at University) when I'm sure I should have been doing something else. When BBC2 broadcast Goal TV last year, I not only sat through the whole thing, but taped it and watched it over and over again. And yes, when we beat Liverpool, I taped every 'Match of the Day' bit involving us, even the 'Nugget' bit.

I failed in every attempt to explain to my friends in London why I am like this - although they came up with some insulting answers - and in a vain attempt to justify my obsession I invited one friend, Nicky, to visit the hallowed ground with me during a weekend visit to Bristol. Well, I did invite her, but friend or otherwise, I was going and she could either come with me or spend the afternoon at home alone. It was November 20, Joe's first match back at the Gate, and it was a derby. A perfect introduction to the mighty reds.

I bought a new T-shirt, and explained each team member from the programme in excessive detail. As far as I can remember, her only reaction was disappointment that Keith Welch was injured (he was featured in the programme). Unfortunately for Nicky, this led to one of my over-preached sermons on how it is not becoming to lust after your own team. This tends to vary a little depending upon how much I have had to drink, as to whether I confess to my own personal stud muffins.

Well, the game began, and soon she was chanting along like a true red, JOE, JOE SUPER JOE ... the first half came and went ... and then they did something I hadn't seen them do this season. They scored. Not a particularly pretty goal, but little Junior had scored. Nicky knew that she had witnessed a miracle and didn't mind a bit as my brother and I went slightly insane. Lo and behold, just as we had calmed down, Wayne gets another, just two minutes later. I couldn't believe it, we were all over them. Just as my brother and I were telling Nicky she had to come to every match as she was obviously a lucky omen, Swindon got one back. Ha ha, said the Swindon fans, that'll teach you ... and then Wayne shut them up with a third. Beautiful. The sheer delight and noise was such that we didn't notice their second go in. And Nicky's reaction? When's the next one?

Nicky didn't actually get to another game, so it is all her fault that we are condemned to the second division (although hopefully for just one season when we can return to first division obscurity). Despite this, she still claims to be a supporter and is now the proud owner of an original circa 1994 scarf.

At least after this game, the journey back up the M4 was a happy, if not hung-over one. I knew I had succeeded when we passed the Swindon junction. After seeing where we were, a small voice next to me whispered, you're so shit it's unbelievable.

Suckers for Punishment

Mark Watson

"The natural state of the football fan is bitter disappointment, no matter what the score," said Nick Hornby, in his fantastic book *Fever Pitch*. Although this truth is universally acknowledged, I wondered constantly while reading the book what Hornby knows about disappointment. What has he had to put up with, as an Arsenal fan for 25 years or thereabouts?

Defeats at Wembley in 1969, '72, '78, '80 and '88. Losing the Cup Winners' Cup Final twice: on penalties in 1980, and to that Nayim goal in the last minute in Paris.

Recently, humiliating FA Cup exits against Wrexham and Millwall, and the fall of George Graham after scarcely-credible allegations. But there has always been generous compensation: a couple of championships (the first won in the most exciting way imaginable), the FA Cup-League Cup double in 1993, the defeat of Parma the year after, and so on. Much as I admire Nick Hornby's exquisite style as a writer, I feel that his standing as an embittered fan must be in doubt. Many fans would be delighted to contend with an Arsenal supporter's problems.

It is the same for fans of every club in football's upper crust. Every time I hear Manchester United supporters cursing their loss of the title by the width of the post Andy Cole hit with the championship in the balance, or Blackburn fans reliving the horror of their hilarious defeat by Swedish part-timers Trelleborg, or Liverpudlians bemoaning their side's long spell without a major trophy (this catastrophic drought has, in fact, lasted just three years, and only then if we discount the Coca-Cola Cup as a serious triumph), I have to restrain an urge to tell them that they simply don't know what it is to suffer for their team.

City fans know what misery is: over the last couple of years our team has allowed us to perfect it, by producing miserable football which last season yielded fewer goals than all but a tiny minority of Endsleigh League clubs. The 1994-95 season will certainly be remembered as City's worst since we nearly disappeared altogether in 1982. My tender age of two caused me to miss a large part of that season, and so nothing could prepare me for the dejection of The Drop.

There had been plenty of heartbreak before, of course, but most of it had at least been heroic heartbreak. The Play-Off Final defeat by Walsall, for example (4-0 in the replay after a 1-3 deficit had been brought back to 3-3 on aggregate, in the days before the one-off decider at Wembley), or England's shoot-out defeat at the hands of West Germany in 1990, after an unexpectedly glorious run to the Semi-Finals of the tournament which had started with a colossally poor 1-1 draw with the Republic of Ireland: they were both shattering disappointments, but there was honour on each occasion. City had earned their chance of promotion with a fine season, while England returned home to a rapturous welcome after wins over Belgium and Cameroon which rank among the most exciting games I have ever seen. In the face of relegation, there was no such consolation, no heroism to hide behind. The jeers of the Premiership supporters at school had to be endured. There could be no defence.

If a day can be pinpointed where City's recent fortunes began the slide which would eventually send them hurtling ignominiously into Division Two, then that day is unquestionably the twentieth of February 1994: a week after my fourteenth birthday. On this sunny afternoon, City led Charlton 1-0 in Round 5 of the FA Cup for at least half-an-hour, before a 20,000 crowd which seems like a figure from the distant past. It had already been a cup run to excite even the most

cynical. Now, in the middle of a depressingly mediocre year, football's pearly gates seemed suddenly to be opening. Then, in the second half, Charlton equalised, and the match ended 1-1. At home, I flung my radio down, knowing instinctively it was all over. The next day, the draw presented "Charlton Athletic or Bristol City" with a trip to Old Trafford. Inevitably, we lost the replay 2-0, and things have never been the same since. It was no consolation, needless to say, when Charlton were easily beaten by a United side in irresistible form. It was no use pretending that City would have gone the same way. We would have beaten them. We knew.

I wasn't there. I wasn't there when the lights went out against Liverpool, because I simply couldn't get a ticket; I wasn't there for the rematch, when they were lucky to escape with a 1-1 draw after a City performance which, in the context of the season as a whole, can only be described as miraculous (when the highlights were on Sportsnight we were praised by Alan Hansen. I have rarely felt so proud in my life), because the tickets went, on the whole, to the same people. I wasn't one of 10,000 delirious fans at Anfield, for City's most unbelievably glorious night for many years (a spokesman from the board called it City's greatest victory ever, but this must be seen as the propaganda of desperate under-achievers), because, obviously, tickets were rarer than cheerful Mondays; I wasn't at the 4-0 trouncing of Stockport, because it was in Stockport; and I wasn't at the Charlton game, because my French Exchange partner arrived, with extraordinarily poor timing, on the same day.

To add to the frustration of the long nights pacing up and down the room to the agitated tones of Alan Green, practically everyone I knew in the World was at at least one of the matches; many were football fans in a purely nominal sense, attracted by the big names on show, who will probably never see a City game again, or at any rate not until Blackburn or Arsenal come to town. The presence of the "fair-weather fan" is exasperating at the best of times. But when they fill the ground at your expense, the usual contempt as you imagine them studying the programme to identify players whom you recognise instinctively, giggling stupidly at the name of Junior Bent because they have never heard of him, and cheering the wrong goals because of their unfamiliarity with the idea of the change kit, mingles with bitter, biting jealousy to create a dark hatred. Fortunately, we true obsessives find ourselves unable to carry on rational thought on any subject during a match - the nervous effort consumed by radio listening is too exhausting - and so the hatred is soon dispelled. All the same, during pauses in Radio Five's commentary, I found myself silently cursing anyone in the crowd who was not singing his or her heart out. What right had they to be there? It was unfair, but fandom is a desperate business.

Attempting to rectify the injustice of our absences from the Liverpool games, I went twice to see City with Steve - a similarly fanatical friend and victim of the fly-by-night fans - in January 1994, and watched the team who were shortly to demolish Liverpool produce 180 minutes of extraordinarily poor football. The first game, a goalless draw with uninspired Stoke City, was the worst match either of us have ever seen - we sat in an empty front row opposite the Dolman Stand, on extremely wet seats, on a miserable day, and shivered and cursed and groaned for the duration of the match, which reached its lowest point when Liam Robinson, a cheerful hard-working striker who turned out to be City's worst signing under Russell Osman, rounded the 'keeper and pushed the ball wide of an unguarded net. (Robinson left at the end of the season with a pitiful haul of five goals; at his new club, Burnley, he was an instant success.) Then, sandwiched between the glorious Liverpool matches, we watched Notts County arrive at Ashton Gate with the division's worst away record and leave with a 2-0 win. "I enjoyed the experience of the game," commented Steve's Mum, who made her debut at the County match. We said nothing. Days later, Liverpool were out of the Cup, Souness was out of a job, and the Stoke and Notts County games were already history. It is my personal belief that medals should be presented to everyone who saw both matches.

With these bitter experiences behind me, I should have seen through the cup run: I should have recognised it as a brief respite from reality, an entertaining sideshow to be enjoyed before we were thrust back into the real world. But, along with everyone else, I was happy to swallow the idea of a renaissance.

We had beaten Liverpool: we could beat anyone. The simple truth is that cup victories, however magnificent, are a misleading picture of a team's prospects. We could have looked at Wrexham, or Woking, or Sutton United to see this. Instead we all believed that things were improving.

So it came as a shock when City hit the bottom six around October 1994 and stayed there, when, looking objectively, we should have been prepared for it. By Christmas, the fans had come to terms with the situation - long before the players and management, who spoke cheerfully of a last-ditch recovery even when it was far, far too late - and begged for something to be done. "Sign a striker," pleaded the supporters, unable to tolerate any further the glaring lack of goals. "Please sign a striker," we persisted, as the months went by and nothing was done. "There's no money to spend," said the board. Less than two years ago, Andy Cole had been sold for £1.7 million. After the last game, a listless 1-2 defeat by Reading where the visitors' goals were greeted by ironic laughter, directors seemed genuinely surprised when season-tickets, and abuse, were hurled in their direction.

Yes, City fans know about misery. And yet, in the middle of a close-season with almost no transfer activity, looking ahead to nine months of games with the likes of Walsall and Shrewsbury, I know that I will be excited on the opening day, as if there were real hope for the future. I know also that, like thousands of others, I will always be a City fan. Perhaps we are all suckers for punishment; or perhaps, as I have always secretly believed, we are all mad.

Summer Fun Football

David Parry Jones, Speedwell Resource and Activity Centre

Boy kicking the football
Down the field
Sunny day, no rain,
Paths, houses, blue sky,
Trees, pond, tennis court,
Badminton.
Kicking the ball high,
People enjoying themselves,
Cheering the teams on,
Scoring goals to win,
Football in the net,
I wish everyday
Was a football day.

Thirty Year Hangover

Steven Leckie

Have you ever woken up with the sort of hangover where your eyes aren't opposite the holes, your mouth feels like a home for retired cheese and overnight somebody left a cannonball in your head? That's not the worst part - oh, no. The absolutely worst thing is when your mind starts clearing enough to put together bits and pieces from the night before. They flash at you at random, making you

chuckle or cringe, or else - and this is the worst bit - you rack your brains and wonder, as though your life depended on it, did I really do that? Did I say that or just think it? It goes round and round wearing grooves in your mind for days on end and you just know that no-one's going to tell you, because by now you can't even remember who was there.

If you know what this is like, then you know how it is to be an English football fan aged thirty-five or over. Not Manchester United against Benfica, not Gordon Banks' miraculous save from Pele (even in slow motion), not Liverpool's extended SAS raid on the silverware of Europe - nothing, nothing can

assuage that existential doubt running through the English psyche like a fault line through Wembley.

July 30th, 1966. Nobby Stiles takes it from the centre circle and sends it away down the right wing, Alan Ball chases it almost to the corner flag and angles it back into the penalty area where Geoff Hurst knocks it down, then twists and falls as he hits it up against the bar. It bounces down behind the keeper and out, Roger Hunt leaps in triumph and Wolfgang Weber heads it clear.

Play it back. Play it again. In slow motion. Backwards. Only the goal line knows for sure, and it isn't going to tell us. If this matters to you like it matters to me, you can write the next bit yourself.

How could it have hit the bar from that angle and not come down behind the line? On the other hand, how could it have come down behind the line and then bounced out? On the other hand, Roger Hunt was perfectly placed to put it in if he'd been in any doubt. On the other hand, how objective is Roger Hunt? If you've ever been a witness in a road accident you know there are parts of your memory that don't add up, however clearly you recall them. No - Roger Hunt doesn't know, and neither does Wolfgang Weber, even if they think they do - they were both high on something more intoxicating than alcohol, we all were, and after the celebrations and the longest hangover in history that niggling, nagging doubt keeps creeping back.

The wilderness years, Maradonna's 'hand of God', the 1990 penalties, the San Marino goal - all of this is bearable only because we're 'Former World Champions England'. We're not also-rans, we're somebody, and nothing can take that away from us. And yet - and yet -

What is the sound of one hand clapping? How does the man who drives the snow-plough get to work? This sentence is a lie, true or false?

At the heart of English football, ten seconds of urgent insolubility: Ball turns it in, Hurst twists and shoots, it rebounds, Hunt leaps, Weber clears; Ball, Hurst, Hunt, Weber.

Play it back. Play it back. Play it back.

Bristol City and Me

Pam Day

"Why support Bristol City? You live the wrong side of town for City." It's true, I have always lived nearer Eastville than Ashton. But then grandpa, a Londoner, who moved to Bristol as a lad, had lived at Bedminster. Ashton Gate was just down the road. It was he who introduced me to football or more specifically Bristol City and after that I could never bring myself to go to Eastville or Twerton unless it was to watch "my team".

So it was that some forty years ago a teacher wrote at the end of an English essay: "This should make interesting reading for the boys". As a junior school pupil I had written a report about a match at Ashton Gate. It featured John Atyeo, Alec Eisentrager and the team of the mid 50s. My early visits to the City ground were with my grandpa and mother. We sat on the ringside and really felt part of the game. On one occasion the ball hit my coat, the mud stayed until it had all worn off! We travelled from Bishopston on a "Football Special". These buses converged on Ashton from all parts of the city, as the family car had not yet made its impact. The drivers and conductors sat in front of the stand (where the Dolman Stand is now) and would leave before the end of the match ready to man the buses for the return journey. Then at six o'clock it was time to buy the Green'un or Pink'un and compare the journalist's view of the match with our own.

It gave me great pleasure as a teenager to make model robins from felt and give them to my favourite players: John Atyeo, John White and Tommy Burden and the rest. I still carry my original robin to every game. I wonder if any others survive?

Then for a time other interests took me away from football but by the time I was in my late teens I had a motor scooter. Ashton Gate now became more accessible. This time I would stand in the Enclosure (now the Lower Williams Stand) sometimes alone and sometimes with my mother. She would ride pillion, much to the amusement of one particular policeman. We had crossed Bedminster Bridge and were ascending Redcliffe Hill when he passed us on his bicycle and shouted a comment relating to the strain we were putting on the scooter! The players I recall from those years are Wally Hinshellwood, Mike Thresher and Bob Anderson.

Again I drifted away - in body if not in spirit - because of family commitments. Then, some years ago the first match of the season fell on my birthday. Where else could anyone want to spend their time, so off we went, my two daughters and I. We stood in the shed and it was great to be back. Following the (annual) pitch invasion we ventured on to the cinder track and acquired a few blades of grass.

In the years since that day both my elder daughter and I have become matchday staff at Ashton Gate. Our duties have included assisting the ground staff by forking the pitch

to make it playable - how else was I ever going to stand in the centre circle and not get fined £400!

Because of this the only way I can watch City now is to travel to away games. The friendly reception we get away from Bristol only goes to show the troublesome element at matches are the minority but unfortunately they receive the publicity. One particularly friendly "person" I met this season was a West Midlands police dog called Jake - who, at the time, was more interested in having his belly tickled than upholding the law. Coincidentally, his handler had been a member of the Junior Reds.

The 1994 FA Cup match at Anfield was a memorable evening: arriving in time to see the team coach deliver the players, walking round the outside of the stadium, the memorial to the Hillsborough Disaster, the Kop, the result and my daughter being escorted to the First Aid room. The excitement of Brian Tinnion's goal on a cold evening had brought on an asthma attack!

What of the future? My ultimate dream must be to watch Bristol City beat Manchester United in the Final of the FA Cup and so avenge that 1909 defeat!

Yesterday's Gladiators

Ron Notton

During the late 1940s and early 1950s I played football for the Bristol Co-op. Our shirts were yellow and black quarters, our home ground at Downend but away fixtures were spread all over Bristol and surrounding area. The Wednesday League was made up of various teams and players, not only shop-workers enjoying their half-day but early starters and shift-workers. The railway, Post Office, firemen, police and roundsmen from bakeries and dairies. Most had done from four to eight hours work before playing. Other teams, like the Army at Horfield Barracks and the RAF at Pucklechurch and Locking, were young and fit and travelled with a coachload of supporters. The standard of the League therefore varied.

One Tuesday, the day before a big match at Durdham Downs, our goal-keeper went down with flu. In a local café we discussed the serious problem when, out of the blue, Bert mentioned that he'd played in goal for his regiment during the war. He'd never shown much interest in playing before but we urged him to turn out despite his modest claim that he wasn't up to professional standard.

Bert had never been modest about his achievements before; tough customers respected him and ensured their bills were paid. Aggressive dogs with sharp teeth whimpered and slunk off when Bert approached. Yet Bert always had the police and authority backing because like those heroes of old, he played a straight bat, he was a good guy.

We should have known better.

When we ran out on to the pitch Bert really looked the part - even to cap and gloves -

although there was no sun and the pitch was bone-dry.

At the kick-in he impressed when dealing with rising shots by making little effort but nonchalantly finger-tipping them over the bar. Unfortunately, during the match, no shots needing this treatment came his way - only the normal pressure, hassle and scrimmages. He proved hopeless at ground shots, fumbled the ball and ran backwards and forwards in a manner that had the rest of us in panic. We got to the stage of having three men on the goal-line. I and the other full-back only left the goal-line to take goal-kicks, Bert's kicking being too weak.

Although play rarely got into the opposing half we managed to keep a clean sheet until after half-time. Then came a series of events that turned the whole game into one to be remembered.

They had a corner but as the winger swung it out too far, our defence naturally came off the goal-line, their tall centre-half went up, meeting the ball with his forehead. Straight away we all knew it was going wide, in fact many of his team-mates started running back. I turned about and saw the ball coming towards me, kicked, I presumed, by one of the spectators, so picked it up for a goal-kick. The referee blew his whistle and pointed to the penalty spot. My mouth dropped open and I made a motion of arms in protest - no surrounding the referee in an aggressive manner in those days - and was told by a spectator that the ball had struck the linesman so had not gone out of play. I was guilty of

hand-ball!

Their centre-half came up to take the penalty, a big chap with boots that looked like packing-cases. Bert didn't crouch like other keepers but stood stiff with extended arms looking like those tin cut-out keepers supplied with a blow-football game when I was a kid.

The ball was blasted over the bar but the referee judged that Bert had moved - actually he'd cringed - so the kick had to be re-taken. Again the ball sailed over with the same re-action, except that Bert cringed to the left instead of the right.

The ball was placed again for the third time. I think by now the whole farce had got to the centre-half and affected his nerve. He mistimed his run-up and stubbed his toe just in front of the ball which moved slowly along the ground towards the goal. Bert sized the situation up in a flash and ran out wildly aiming a mighty kick, but missed.

The ball just made it over the line.

In those days players didn't do handstands or kiss each other when a goal was scored. They looked jubilant and shook hands. On this occasion there was silence. The players moved up for the kick-off as if assembling for a funeral.

There were more goals against us after but not as many as we'd feared. I think the other side felt a little shame-faced.

We'd had our photo taken before the match. We are all looking so confident, with Bert, arms folded, looking like Superman. I wonder if he shows that photo to his sons and family?

I also wonder if, like my sons, they look at our hair styles, those clumpy boots with the hard toes and shapeless socks with thick American magazines stuffed in them for shin-guards. Look at our roomy, baggy shorts that reached down to our knees and then snigger?

Natural Gas

Martin Barker

Sunday afternoon. The station.
Two hours late to platform nine.
End of a portentous journey -
early season expectations
rescued by a last-gasp winner,
never certain if we'd make it,
last, a train that nearly didn't -
still, we've made it now. Two gasheads
walking up and feeling fine.
Walking past the northern banners,
past the early chants and hand-claps,
holding butterflies at bay,
hope and nervousness assembling,

tonsils limbered up and trembling,
turning into Wembley Way.

Here, like almost premonitions,
little puffs of sound, smoke signals,
tiny snatches of rehearsal,
notes and phrases enter play ...
... Irene goodnight ...Irene ... see you
in my dreams ...
yeah!

Mostly though, a buzz of greetings:
two meet four become six hundred
multiply to thirty thousand
gathering a choral plainsong
welcoming in rich crescendo ...

... the match.
And living the agony at last. Becoming, no
being the team. And soon, after the early
roar and blood and guts and thunder,
it settles, we settle into a
first half pattern: hurting.
Balls in the air over the Rovers goal,
hearts in mouths, outer and inner turmoil.
No pattern to our yells, unable to find
a space, or pace. Couplets
desperately passed in one-touch stanzas
that break down: rhythm astray at the caesura.
Pressure. Rare sorties to the metric line.
Then backpedal, hold them glottally at the
back-stop.
More pressure.
Finally, inevitably, they scored.

Children in the park can do it.

Strikers showing off can do it.
Get the ball up, head to forehead,
never let it touch the soil.
Andy Booth, their golden striker,
he's the one with star potential
(Liverpool will surely take him)
he could do it, he can do it,
joins the game of keep-it-up-there,
breaks the rules, and heads for ... goooal!!!!

You know the film Battle of Britain? Near the
end, there's
one climactic scene where the cloudless sky's
alive with planes
pirouetting and turning impossible circles,while
every now and
then one twists in pain and exits in a trail of
dark smoke. And
there's no sound. It's all shot in silence, a
noiseless death
dance. In my memory, that's how I see that
goal: ears closed
totally down, but all eyes. Then the
Huddersfield crowd split
that sky, mercilessly. And we're stunned.

To the breach comes Marcus Stewart -
young, doe-eyed, wild-haired and headband,
precious boy, precocious assets -
feels the pain as play resumes.
Sees the awful situation,
reads the dreadful situation,
sees a hopeful cross that hangs up,
gets it neatly nodded down,
turns on a proverbial sixpence,
finds an inch and volleys home ...

Now the total paroxysm,
now the Rovers crowd's delirium,
hopes rekindled, passions boundless.
Then as throats pass through the spasm,
hear the cry of "You're not singing
anymore" reverberate!
When the referee's squawk signals
quarter hour's release of tension;
once again with energetic
cosmic force, our chords vibrate:

IRENE GOODNIGHT IRENE,
IRENE HALF TIME
GOODNIGHT IRENE
YOU'RE GREAT IRENE
WE'LL SING YOU TILL THE TEAMS
COME OUT AGAIN.
And in the second half, it's as if Irene's dream
had come to life, totally, here at Wembley.
Rovers found the parts two seasons hadn't
reached - where the bloody hell's the midfield?
- and they play it.
Balls pass from space to man to space with
numbing brilliance, leaving the opposition
sucking air: hudsucker mudboys grasping at
slippy straws. Oh, we trojanhorsed their
defences
and ran clefts through all of them. This was
such engrossing wonderfulness -
the beautiful game: a precis, by Bristol Rovers.
With real pride we sang, in rhythm with slick
moves:

IRENE GOOD FLIGHT TO THE WING
DRILLED BACK JUST RIGHT,
A LOW ONE-TOUCH CROSS-SHOT INSWINGS,
IS FINISHED IN MY DREAMS ...

45

But then gradually and as tides inexorably turn
and rise,
the average height of passes climbed: chest,
shoulder, head,
and Huddersfield came blundering back at us.
Dully, inevitably, they came,
gatecrashing the good party.
Goal.
Boring. Bad example to children. Don't let
your
mother see you charging in like that. Thud.
Goal.
Ten minutes to go.

It can't be said we didn't try. We SANG.
I saw young boys and girls weeping and
shouting
all at once. I personally foamed at the mouth
with straining at the bitterness.
The team stayed full on song too, never gave
up.
Together, we took the pitch by the throat, and
dervished.
Ten, nine, seven, two minutes to prevent the
unforgiveable. And then, with one to go,
young Marcus Stewart hit the perfect note.
Swerved, swivelled, ran the face of the
defence,
hoisted an unstoppable shot from an
impossible angle,
twenty five yards out, just one minute from
time ...

A month later, Irene still dreams of that ball.
One month later, long since put away, the
woodwork

quivers with shame. It only had to raise its
chin
in stiff acknowledgement of a brilliant strike
for the ball to pass inside.
Even it could have lifted out of the ground
in a paean of praise, as we did, as we began
to...

Instead it stood and rang like an overtested
tuning fork, the ball returned to play,
was blasted wide and we were left in
                    s
                        h
                            a
                        r
                d
                s.

Do not blame young Marcus Stewart,
do not blame brave Brian Parkin,
Billy Clark or Andy Tillson;
do not blame these honest players,
blame the singer, not the song.
Sing their praise to soothe their anguish
bawl the pain out, raw and strong:

IRENE GOODNIGHT IRENE,
IRENE GOODNIGHT.
GOODNIGHT IRENE,
GOODNIGHT MY TEAM,
I'LL SEE YOU THROUGH THE STREAMS

of folks going chilly home. Pancaked,
Lifted, tossed so high, flattened on impact
All bubbles burst.

Monday lunchtime, Tesco's, Eastville,

waiting for the open bus.
Blue and White returned to Bristol
put its claim of love on us.
Probably goodbye to Marcus,
probably a long hiatus,
start the long rebuilding process -
winters hugged against promotion,
springtime dry with broken Cup dreams,
Wembley watched through long binoculars -
still it puts its claim on us.
This is still the time of heroes,
stuff of legends, stuff of dreams,
here amid the shopping baskets,
young and old and barmy army,
male and female, loving gasheads,
all together crooned the anthem
softly to the glorious team ...

Irene goodnight Irene ...
Irene goodnight ...
goodnight Irene ...
good night Irene ...
I'll see you in my ...

dreams.

If Life has no Meaning, Maybe You Need a Goal

Ben Clapp

I have played football for as long as I can remember, but it hasn't been long enough yet. I have always felt I deserved to play in a "not the best, but not the worst" kind of way.

Football to me is the dream game which runs through my head. The reason I play is that the more I do play, the more often I feel the dream is happening to me, in a pass, in a tackle and occasionally in a goal. These peak experiences, the most golden moments, are timeless and I love them.

When I watch football on the television, I'm secretly revising, looking for the method that will make it happen to me and although I am a long way from the dream game, I can recognise it in others.

This recognition manifests itself in my hero, Ian Rush. There is something about his presence that even his magnificently ugly moustache cannot diminish. At home I have a special long stick which I call the "Urger" and I use it when Ian Rush plays; pushing his predatory on-screen image upfield, poking any players who foul him in their eye, urging the ball to him, waiting to see "Rushy magic". Ian is simply the ripple in the path of the ball which causes it to go into the back of the net. Sometimes it seems as if he hates to interfere with the game, luckily he was born to.

Only one other player ever achieved equal status. That player was Kenny Dalgleish. When I was young I actually thought he was Luke Skywalker, such was his mysterious power. Once, a like-minded child showed me a special position that Kenny held his hands in when he was playing. I did it as often as possible, things haven't really improved, I suppose.

When I play, I feel I know what to do, I chase the dream, like a dumb dog after a stick. With a hopeful fixed expression I run and wait for ninety minutes desperate for a bite. Mostly it just half happens, not failing, just half of what it could be. But I'm sure I'm getting better and every so often it all goes right ...

... So as I run with the ball I'm entering the box from the right. I feign a shot, using the defender's instinctive wincing to slow him, I dart to the left, tapping the ball with my right foot. After two strides I swing with my left, the leg is loose but strong and my boot feels heavy like a sledge-hammer. It arcs around perfectly and the slight hook of my left foot takes the ball up and right with a left curve and so, though the goal keeper dives well, all he can do is a ten digit point to the place in the top corner where the ball has been levered into the net. Life can be a dream come true.

Football Crazy

Brenda Dimond

The Centre placed the football
  steady, ready to be kicked.
In the stands above it all,
  busy knitting needles clicked.

To a man they rose around her
  roaring fit to wake the dead;
she rubbed her aching shoulder
  and fixed earphones on her head.

Poor mum had sadly whispered
  when they read the wedding bans,
'Grass widows come from stupid girls
  who marry football fans.'

She had been a perfect wife
  doing everything she could
to bring him to his senses
  never was it any good.

Whatever crisis happened,
  illness, death or just fatigue,
their lives were regulated
  by arrangement with the League.

The years slowly ground away,
  theirs was not a life of bliss
for muddy football heroes
  were the only ones he'd kiss.

At last, he bought a ticket
  for that turnstile in the sky,
secretly she gave a cheer
  as she waved football 'Bye-bye'

Her joy was much too early
  she was football's victim still
for he had left conditions
  plainly stated in his will.

A legacy was hers to spend
  but here's the wicked catch
to earn it she must attend
  each week the soccer match.

If she failed to see the game
  then the club would get it all.
So every week, rain or shine,
  she went crazy for football.

Over the Moon

Hugh Thomas

A friend of mine is the secretary of a local amateur football team, whom we will call The Wanderers. Embroiled as they were in their annual relegation crisis, their problems on the field were made worse by several longstanding players retiring, leaving the area or being poached by other clubs. I found myself pressed into service to make up the team.

An avid follower of the game on TV and live for many years, I naturally jumped at the chance. My physical qualifications for selection, though, were unimpressive. I had reached the age of 31 without ever having pulled on a football shirt in anger. Not even for my boyhood village primary school team, who regularly had to borrow players from the opposition to make the numbers up.

Even so, I always fancied myself as a striker at school but, rather weak and weedy with spectacles, I never caught the selectors' eye. After that, my football career was suppressed further at a secondary school where we were force-fed rugby. "Football," the games teacher would never tire of telling us, "is a game for gentlemen played by hooligans, while rugby is a game for hooligans played by gentlemen." I

played twice for the second XV, without once touching the ball.

The Wanderers' match, an away game, took place on a cow dung pitch on a breezy hilltop near Village Green, our opponents of the day. Although the crowd comprised only two men, this was, undeniably, a proper match. There was a referee in official black outfit complete with whistle, as well as proper goal posts with real nets. No arguing here whether the ball was inside the heaps of jerseys and coats.

I was assigned the role of striker, on the basis that up there I could do the least damage. As a non-registered player, I was also issued with an assumed name in case I was booked.

Lining up in the centre circle for kick-off I eyed the opposition warily. Would there be any Vinny Joneses singling me out for scything late tackles? The nearest opponent, rubbing his hands together in the cold, appeared distinctly unthreatening. He looked about forty-five, with a bleached Dennis Law-style haircut, and was so short he would have been drowned even in my shirt.

The game began with a shrill pheep from the ref, and we kicked off. A series of midfield scrambles and long aimless punts up and down the field ensued. Then Village Green built a promising attack down their left wing, and eager for an early score with the slope and strong wind in their favour, all pressed forward. Suddenly, though, the move broke down as our full back won the ball and sent it up to the right winger.

Jinking past his man, he streaked up the wing

while I tried to keep up through the middle. Finding his way barred by the single defender who had stayed back, the winger checked, looked around, saw me in the centre and passed. Suddenly I found myself with the ball at my feet, onside, with only the goalie to beat. I neatly controlled the ball with what team mates later told me were four deft touches, and looked up. Without thinking, I lashed the ball goalwards with my left foot.

Before the keeper, or in truth, I knew what had happened, the ball hit the back of the net. One-nil. What a screamer from Hugh Thomas.

I whirled away to accept the acclaim of my team-mates, for a moment as stunned as our opponents.

Of course, Village Green went on to run in double figures at our end. Shorty ran rings round us all for the next 85 minutes, and our rookie goalkeeper let in everything that so much as trickled in his direction. Even the ref laughed out loud at one particularly ludicrous own goal by our centre half.

But although the ball rarely came my way for the rest of the game - and when it did I fell over it - I floated around the pitch on a wave of euphoria. This was finally it, I realised - at last, I knew what it meant to be over the moon.

Football

Margaret Hanstead

This spectator sport
is a religion.
The crowd, involved,
perform their sacred rites
shrieking in adulation
as, arms aloft,
they ripple a Mexican wave
around the packed pavilion
or rattle toys, hold banners high,
shake their strip scarfs
to show allegiance.

In matching tones their team
covers the pitch
young men's barelegs
mud-streaked, flailing,
running the course
and when the ball
is punched into goal -
by foot or head -
the pack embrace hysterically
and the hero sinks to his knees
in prayer.

Friday May 23 1986

R. Crane

Friday May 23 1986 started like any other day but it didn't finish like it for me. It was the day before Bristol City, the team I had supported since I was in short trousers, were to finally appear at that Mecca of football - Wembley Stadium. Nobody cared that it was to contest the Freight Rover Trophy, with the additional prize of a Sherpa Minibus, it was Wembley that was important. These days even teams with no grounds of their own and very little else get there but back in 1986 it was something special.

The faithful followers of the Robins - and several thousand unfaithful supporters, hangers-on, sensation seekers, day-trippers and the odd Gas-Head - were booked to go to Wembley in the morning.

I have always loved Bristol City and maybe I always will so I had vowed at an early age never to attend a match at Wembley until my team ran out there. So at various stages in my life I passed up opportunities to watch the masters of football: Charlton, Best, Maradonna, Eusebio, Rivera, Netzer, DiStefano, Kempes, Beckenbauer - the lot. No, I would have to wait for a City team to make it and during the dark years when City swept majestically from Div 1 to the basement of Div 4 and nearly disappeared altogether, it was hardly an everyday concern! So I succumbed. I was unfaithful. Clandestine Wednesday nights as various England teams tried to qualify for various tournaments. No, I wouldn't watch other club sides, that would be too depraved; I just caught the occasional glimpse of a Brazilian samba, or a Hungarian waltz and the deft skills of English tap dance masters such as Peter Storey, Ian Gillard or Stuart Pearce.

So at 8 pm on Friday May 23 I was not prepared to watch my wife being wheeled into the back of an ambulance outside my home. She had been finding it increasingly difficult to breathe and the doctor suspected acute pneumonia so the ambulance was called, oxygen administered and my wife whisked off to be incarcerated in the BRI. I was obviously greatly concerned. Would this mean I couldn't go to the match? I would have to visit her in hospital and look after our three sons, Duncan, Matthew and Sam. What a dirty, late tackle. I think the worry must have shown in my face because as Lyn, my wife, was being stretchered off into the back of the ambulance she pulled off the oxygen mask and croaked "You... must ... go ... to ... the ... match." "Ok!" I said.

The following morning, in order to make the 9.30 rendezvous for the Executive (suits and ties only/picnic hampers/boxes of wine/barbecue suite) Minibus, I had to be at the BRI bright and early to establish in which ward the Health Authority had hidden my wife overnight. I found it and resplendent in my suit and City tie, red and white rosette and City scarf, I hurried to her bedside. She looked better. Were those roses in her cheeks? Or was it all the red reflecting around her? Anyway, my own little midfield dynamo repeated her command that I should go to the match. Her mother and sister had been alerted and would take care of our boys all day until I returned. "It could be late, Lyn." I said, "some of the lads might want to make a night of it."

"That's all right, they won't mind. Just try to ring them and let them know when you'll be home," Lyn said. "Will do, luv," I shouted over my shoulder as I disappeared down the hospital corridor to sprint round the corner to catch the minibus at the pre-arranged point a few streets away. So the day was still as planned: Bristol - Membury Services - Breakfast/Bucks Fizz - M4 - Ealing Common - Barbecue lunch/wine - Wembley/match - London/beer - Home.

It didn't go smoothly. All the coaches, buses, minibuses and most of the cars in Bristol were heading east along the M4 that sunny morning. We managed the breakfast and Bucks Fizz, but then got caught in the heavy traffic, which was surprising really as the hard shoulder was being used as an unofficial additional lane. Arriving late at Ealing Common, we only had time for a picnic, no barbie and a few boxes of wine and some cans of beer.

The game went to plan, we absorbed some early pressure from Bolton but we eventually were worthy winners 3-0. Bolton had a lively winger called Mark Gavin, whom I'd seen play in Leeds Utd's youth team. "Biffo" Newman kicked him a few times and he disappeared. When the final whistle came, Wembley became the cathedral of football I always knew it was. The fans stood and sang, the lads ran up the steps and lifted the cup and they ran round the track dancing, with us all going mad - how else can you describe crying and laughing and having a quasi-religious experience all at the same time?

A few beers in the local hotel, a swift barbie in a local park and then the plan was to round off the day by visiting the West London hotel being used by the team. We had connections; we had an ex-City player, the brother-in-law of a director and several promising members of the 51 Club Old Farts youth section with us. We got in. We were actually in the same room as those players who had played so beautifully on Wembley's lush turf only a few hours before. We were shaking them by the hand, we were hugging them, we touched the trophy, we kissed players, officials, their relatives and above all we drank and we sang.

In all the celebrations no one noticed (how could we from cloud 9?) that our designated return-trip driver was also drinking and singing and now he was starting on sleeping. Ok, so we weren't going to be leaving to schedule, we went back to drinking and singing again. I rang home to speak to mother-in-law. She already knew the result but the joyous, tuneful noises from that hotel lounge could have confirmed it for her.

"Not able to leave just yet," I shouted above the din, "Driver trouble."

As I was speaking the designated one was sitting opposite me having the contents of a jug of black coffee poured into his stomach.

"Could be some time ... " I said.

"Don't worry," said ma-in-law, "It's already one in the morning and I'm sleeping here now. I'll see you when you arrive home."

"Thanks" was all I could say, and six and a half hours later I managed to say it to her face.

We were Crap

Richard Waller

The team I played for as a kid were crap. There is no disputing it, Hill United Under 12's and Under 13's in 1976/77 and 1977/78 were rubbish. I know it is a common feature of being a football fan to privately admit your heroes from Saturday may not be quite the team you suggested they were to the opposition, but we were genuinely crap.

We played in the impressively sounding Thundermite League, our home ground being on Canvey Island, next to a muddy creek. We finished bottom of our league both seasons, winning just once and managing a couple of draws in two years. The ethos of the club was definitely the Olympian creed that taking part is more important than winning, but such admirable Corinthian notions cut little ice in the school playground on a Monday morning.

All of the lads who played for teams on a Sunday would get together to compare results at break-time and this soon became the worst time of the week for me and my team-mates. Whilst the kids who played for the likes of the Dynamos or Hadleigh Town could recount how they ventured into deepest Basildon and managed to battle out a 2-1 victory over the feared lads of Holy Trinity, those of us from Hill United had to admit to a 14-0 drubbing at the hands of Aztec Boys or Vange.

We rapidly became the laughing stock of the football players, a source of humour for those who saw football as something to WIN, not just a recreation to be enjoyed. We couldn't lie about the result, since the local newspaper printed all of the scores on a Tuesday evening. No, we had to face up to the fact that our team was crap.

Looking back, the person I feel most sorry for is our goalkeeper. Whilst us outfield players could hide on the wide expanse of a pitch (I strolled around endeavouring to emulate the silky skills of Glen Hoddle from the centre of midfield) the poor goalie was unable to go anywhere else. That said, he brought much of the frequent criticism on himself - he was barely able to clear the penalty box with a goal kick, nor get anywhere near halfway with a drop kick. During the course of an average game, he'd perform acts that would, if repeated in the 'professional arena' bring about an FA enquiry into possible match rigging. He would leave balls obviously bound for the back of the net, or shout "Yours!" if any unfortunate defender happened to be in the six yard box.

Whilst this was frustrating for the rest of the team, it seemed to be worse for the half a dozen dads who faithfully showed up every week to relive their long lost youthful days by yelling and bawling at those of us in green and black stripes. Some dads got to act as linesmen on occasion, but that rarely stopped them 'coaching', and probably led to their frequently dubious decisions with the flag. Several fathers were appreciated, though, for more practical reasons. Indeed, despite our manager's relaxed attitude towards success on the pitch, some of his stranger team selections

probably arose from a player's father being willing to leave his bed and drive to Tilbury or Pitsea on a cold Sunday morning in February. Whilst such selection decisions are unlikely to plague a professional manager, I cannot help but wonder whether Lee Dixon's Dad is the FA's team coach driver. Why else would he have played for England so often?

Now that my participation in football is limited to an occasional game of 5-a-side, the memories are generally good ones. Despite the frequent humiliations and the embarrassment of wearing plastic boots with moulded studs until I had saved enough paper round money for a pair of size 5 Beckenbauer Supers, there were good times too. A thundering 10-yard shot which would have pulled the score back to 4-1 against Stamford Juniors (disallowed as offside as our centre forward, Brian, was tying up his boot laces on the goal-line), a mazy run where I beat three players before executing a pin-point 30 yard pass which led to a rare goal for our team, and vivid memories of playing against a star of the future.

Whilst my dad can claim to have been in an infant school team opposite Jimmy Greaves and my uncle was in the same school side as Terry Venables, I too played against a top-flight pro. Stewart Robson - until recently captain of Coventry City after failing to make the grade at West Ham and Arsenal - played for the mighty Aztecs, and directly against me in the battle for midfield control. If memory serves, in one game we lost 19-0 and he scored 5. Still, I don't hold it against the guy, and have had him in my Fantasy Football team for the last few seasons - for old time's sake, for Hill United, even if we were crap.

Partisanship

Ian Layne

Partisanship between supporters of Bristol City and Bristol Rovers is legendary but my acquaintance Albert carried this even further. Any club other than his beloved Bristol City was the object of his scorn and derision.

Albert was a mild mannered birdlike man of diminutive stature. Except on match days when he was transformed into a giant and a fury. Whenever a football was kicked in earnest at Ashton Gate Albert would be there, whether for a first team match, reserves or friendly. In his usual spot on the front row of the terraces, near the half way line, he acted as the self appointed scourge of the visiting team, heaping vituperation on its players.

On principle Albert never travelled to City's away matches as paying admission at the turnstiles of any other ground would be tantamount to directly subsidising a rival club.

Albert and his wife acquired a lodger from somewhere up-country who had no interest in football whatsoever. He preferred to spend his Saturday afternoons browsing around Bristol and was always back for Saturday tea by the time Albert returned from a match. However, on one particular Saturday the club from his home town were playing the Rovers at Eastville and some of the lodger's relatives were travelling with the team's supporters. The lodger took the opportunity of going over to the Rovers' ground to meet up with them and in consequence was absent from his usual place at table. Albert's wife innocently mentioned the reason for his absence. When the lodger returned later that evening his neatly packed suitcases were standing on the garden path.

Misses

Lee Bryant

I knew if Rovers didn't beat Huddersfield at Wembley I wouldn't get the job. I tried to kid myself that it wasn't the case but some turning part of my stomach knew.

We had to win. If there was any justice then we had to win. We had no ground, no money, just determination and Marcus Stewart. What if they did have a spanking new ground and a natural Darth Vader if ever there was one in Neil Warnock? Other reasons why we were going to win were that City had gone down and Miller's goal against Crewe had secured our place at Wembley. If goals like that win you a place at Wembley then it's clearly your season. So we were going to win and I was going to get the job.

I stayed with friends in London. On the trip up I tried to remember whether this was good or bad. Had Rovers won the games I'd seen when I'd stayed with them before? I couldn't remember. My friends thought I was rather off the whole stay. They're not football fans.

Sunday morning, match day and oh no ... I haven't got anything blue to wear. Well, it's blue but striped and Huddersfield play in stripes. It wouldn't matter, it was all superstitious nonsense. Wearing a striped shirt wouldn't affect the team's performance just as the team's performance wouldn't affect my interview. If all that's true why did I feel as uncomfortable as Terry Venables in the same room as Alan Sugar?

I got to the designated pub along with a couple of hundred Rovers and Huddersfield fans. They were sat outside. I walked up to the door and pushed and nothing. It was quarter to twelve, the pubs didn't open till twelve, Sunday opening, not a good omen. I stood next to the Rovers' contingent. And waited.

And waited. My uncle and his mates were supposed to be here the same time as me, most importantly so was my ticket. The pub opened and I managed to push my way to the bar. The beer I wanted was off. Just another nail in the coffin. Luckily, at that point my friends turned up, no sign of Unc or my ticket, but at least I could push my doom-laden thoughts aside for a while.

Then my brothers turned up. My brothers who'd travelled up from Bristol that day as opposed to my Uncle who was staying with friends in London. I began to shiver even though it wasn't a warm day like a character in a James Herbert novel. Then suddenly Unc was there and so were his mates and so were our tickets.

It was time to enjoy the day. To sing a few songs and sink a few pints. At one stage we became a tourist sight. God only knows who the Japanese thought we were but we were happy to oblige them with poses. Everybody admitted they hadn't thought about the outcome of the game.

I think we outsang and outplayed Huddersfield. Sure, they had most of the possession in the first half but we had the clearer chances. They scored with a few minutes of the first half left. It was like someone had died. Then Stewart, the outstanding player of the game, scored an equaliser and the Ref blew for the end of the half. We were going to make it.

We dominated the second half. Gareth Taylor missed a sitter. If he plays football for a hundred years he'll never miss another chance as easy as that one. Stewart went close, oh so close, so many times. Then they scored. I can't remember the exact time but there was only a few minutes left and still we advanced. Browning went close and Stewart again but it wasn't to be.

On the tube back my Uncle's mate looked like a child whose favourite toy has been thrown on the bonfire and not the company director he is. Nobody spoke. It was horrible. Why couldn't they have won? Why couldn't they have won?

My brothers had parked at Ealing. We walked round, tried to find somewhere to eat. We ended up at McDonalds as nowhere else was open. We all ordered the same thing and had to wait ages for it and the Fanta was flat. It seemed an appropriate end to the day.

On the way back my brother got lost. When was the day of hell ever going to end? Eventually we got on to the motorway. Near Swindon a car with the scarves and stickers was ahead of us. As we passed a boy, six or seven, with the kit on waved. He looked so happy.

Then something even more wonderful happened. What was this up ahead? It couldn't be? It was. The team coach. As we passed we waved like idiots. Gareth Taylor looked suicidal but still managed to wave. I felt so sorry for him. Then we overtook the coach and looked back and waved. John Ward, yes, John Ward waved and smiled at us. It was all going to be okay.

The job? Nope didn't get it but I have sent off my forms for my season ticket. Can't be unlucky two seasons in a row, we just can't.

They call me Superstitious- Bristol Man wins World Cup Match for England

Alan Tanner

They call me superstitious. But they don't understand. I've gone beyond the simple stuff like wearing certain clothes on match days, or following pre-match rituals to secure success

for the team. No, I've gone into the realms of psychic powers.

Have you noticed how frequently the other team score when your attention has been distracted for a moment? Have you noticed how a confident statement about the near future like "Well, City's through to the next round now" often comes before an amazing comeback by the opposition? How many of you have come away from a match like me burdened with the certain knowledge that it is you who are responsible for that stunning last minute goal that defeated City?

Well, I have harnessed these connections between thought, deed and chance. By taking advantage of my observations about how to manipulate apparently chance events, I have achieved some notable successes.

Take for example that game at The Hawthorns between City and West Bromwich towards the end of what was to be City's promotion season to Division 1. West Brom were also in the promotion race. A win would mean very likely promotion, a draw would keep things fragile, and a loss would mean a struggle. The first half turned out to be a tense and dour affair with few chances. Just before half-time my friend Dave said "I'm going to get a pastie."

Now, I must say here that my football friends have developed similar powers to me. This is strange because you must never talk about them before, during or after a game, or risk disaster. Their use cannot be planned either. So co-operative effort is difficult to achieve.

So, when Dave announced his intention to go and get a pastie, I dreaded that he was going to add " that'll make it happen," but he was skilled enough to keep quiet. However, my father who is sceptical about these powers, began to say something. I knew it would be something to the effect that a goal would be sure to result. So did my friend Steve, and between us we managed to keep him quiet by pointing out how the corner flags all flew in the same direction unlike the ones at opposite ends on the Dolman Stand side of the pitch at Ashton Gate.

By the time Dave returned it was half-time and Gerry Sweeney had seen his speculative long range shot creep into the top corner of the net to put City 1-0 up.

In the second half we had to use our emergency back-up weapon - Steve's hat. He very rarely wore this woollen hat however cold it was, but kept it in his pocket. West Brom took over the game in the second half and particularly in the last fifteen minutes threw in attack after attack so that a score seemed inevitable. Ten minutes from the end out came the hat. Steve put it on. I'm sure that he, like myself, was fearful that this tinkering with the course of time and events would end in tears. However, City held out in a way that can only feebly be described as unbelievable. Right at the end, full-back Donny Gillies was knocked unconscious to the ground making a goal-line block. The ball bounced around in the six-yard box before being propelled powerfully net-wards. As this happened, Donny was lifting himself in a daze from the ground. The ball hit him again and bounced to safety. I hope you can see why such power has to be used so sparingly.

My greatest greatest feat was when I decisively influenced a game in Italy from my home in Bristol. Remember the World Cup in Italy in 1990 and the impact that Nigeria had on the tournament? The quarter-finals had England playing Nigeria. Now, the Nigerians had in their camp a very worthy opponent indeed. He didn't play, but he did successfully predict all the scores of their games in the World Cup and, I understand, several before. His prediction for the quarter-final was Nigeria 2, England 1. Steve and I were worried.

Our worries were confirmed. There were fifteen minutes to go and the score was Nigeria 2, England 1. Furthermore, it seemed that England could not make an impact on the game. What could I do?

The ball went out near the halfway line for an England throw. The ball bounced toward the England bench. Here was my chance! I plaited together all the strands of my thoughts, I wound up the psychic power supply and focussed sharply. It worked! Amazingly, the England bench caught the ball, but threw back (to Platt, I think) a different ball! England changed the ball! With the 2-1 ball off the pitch England went on to win 3-2 (one of their goals a penalty).

Incidentally, people at work who don't normally watch football thought I was crazy when I pointed all this out. But once the video recording that one of them had made was checked and the incident confirmed, they looked at me in a different light. Perhaps I should have missed out the bit about my role in it.

Now, if I remind you that in the next round, England lost after a penalty shoot-out, you may well suggest that the enormity of my feat in the Nigeria match had depleted my powers. Well, I admit it's a possibility, but I don't think so. I must now record publicly my sincere apologies to Chris Waddle. As he prepared to take that fateful kick, my attention was distracted momentarily by a distant siren. While I was re-focussing, I had a vision of the ball rising high over the goal and going into the crowd. Chris Waddle was helpless. He kicked the ball implausibly high over the net.

It doesn't worry me that they call me superstitious. I am a little concerned about this last season gone by, though. It goes without saying that I did not perform well, and I shall spare you the grisly details. Still, the reverses I suffered mean that the powers are taking a re-charge. There's a new season coming up full of possibilities. I for one will be working hard to limit the losing possibilities and secure the winning ones.

Football Perspective

Mark Wenham

Perhaps the most vivid and lasting image of the Lansdowne Road Soccer Riot was the sight of James Eager, blond, angelic and only eight years old, clutching his father for safety as England's hooligans hurled their seats on to the pitch.

Sitting at home watching events unfold on Sky TV with a six-pack of beer and my own son for company, I certainly felt a strong, parental empathy and, in the frightened, tear-filled eyes of the boy himself imagined I saw a symbol of innocence lost, of reality barging its way into a child's world.

I also found myself wondering how, in the event of a re-start, England's centre-halves would cope now that Row Z had been transferred to ground-level.

Things were considerably less traumatic in our lounge, though the 'Night of Shame' claimed two further casualties when my sixteen-month-old son was caught ripping out pages from two old 'Shoot' albums while the Stewards' backs were turned, and I was cautioned by my wife for hurling invective at the TV screen. I explained to her that a chance to share my anger and frustration might help, which is how, some time into my fourth can of lager, I came to be delivering a diatribe on the merits of public flogging to an audience comprising Mickey Mouse, Big Ted and Flipper the wind-up plastic dolphin.

At which point, all alone in the room, I heard myself say "You see, it was different when I was a lad ..."

And, with the stadium empty now, save for the English support and the Riot Police, I remembered my first ever game and a conversation with my father two Christmases ago.

We'd both recently finished reading *Fever Pitch* by Nick Hornby and, well into our third bottle of wine, were reminiscing about the games we attended together during the 1970s.

Actually, that's not strictly true. I was reminiscing while my Dad, with his teflon-coated recall for names and places, was stabbing around for inspiration.

I took him by the arm and guided him gently down memory lane.

First stop was Highbury and my first ever live game. It was an eighth birthday treat and I saw Arsenal versus Huddersfield Town. I remembered the singing, the smells and the greenness of the grass. We saw George Graham giving away unsolicited gifts in midfield, Charlie George coming on at the same time as the floodlights, and Bob Wilson, the goalie, showing a fearlessness which already hinted at a potentially great autocue technique. To that date it was the most exciting day of my life. John Radford scored the only goal of the game. One nil to the Arsenal.

I recalled a game between Arsenal and Liverpool, Highbury packed to the rafters with 58,000 fans, and Arsenal in carnival mood, winning by two goals to nil. Alan Ball, worried that his squeaky voice, red hair and diminutive stature didn't make him immediately recognisable, was wearing kinky white leather soccer boots. He scored both goals, the second from the penalty spot which my Dad, the most pessimistic of fans, would have put the mortgage on him missing. We both shut our eyes. I opened mine just in time to see the ball placed low and hard into the bottom right corner of the net. "No problem. Never

doubted him," said my father with a straight face.

Best of all - and most luminous of my boyhood sporting memories - was seeing the great Liam Brady in his pomp, orchestrating a 3-1 home thumping of Manchester United.

Throughout the game my Dad kept telling me how Malcolm MacDonald, who scored twice, used to play right back for Tonbridge, but was forced to switch position because his bow legs made him too easy to nut-meg.

I wasn't listening. I was entranced. Liam Brady was the nearest I came to a fully fledged boyhood crush. I was devastated when the romance ended and he packed his bags for foreign climes.

I sat back in my chair, wiped a tear from my eye, and asked my father to share with me his recollections of those self-same games.

I figured this would take all of thirty seconds, and I was just about to suggest opening another bottle of wine, when he leaned forward and spoke.

"Actually there are two main things I remember." He paused for effect.

"The Fighting - and the Swearing."

And he was off, exploding myths like Darwin at a church social.

He remembered the camaraderie in the days before segregation, when you could stand among a group of large Huddersfield fans, jot down your Last Will and Testament on a team sheet, and pray to God that the little bloke shouting questions like "Why are all Yorkshiremen fairies?" wouldn't turn round and address you as Dad.

He recalled, chillingly, Arsenal versus Liverpool and the same crowd of 58,000, but with people crushed together so tightly they couldn't breathe. He told of the smell of fear, of Mums and Dads trying not to panic, and of frightened rumours spreading that they still hadn't closed the gates. He harked back to the joys of dragging a baffled child from one end of a terrace to another in an attempt to find a suitable vantage point for a midget, of sidling past skinheads learning to swear by rote, and of the outdoor pub league where people practised darts and shove ha'penny without using boards.

He remembered 200 Manchester United fans trying to take the North Bank, pitched battles spilling on to the pitch, policemen lying injured, and having to stand with his arms around me whilst the fights rumbled round us.

Finally, he reminded me of the ridiculous cost of white schoolboy soccer boots endorsed by Alan Ball, and as a coup de grace, assured me that after watching Liam Brady doss around for 90 minutes my schoolboy soccer career had gone to pot.

All of which says a great deal about perspective, and makes me wonder how many falling trees and runaway trains I blithely ignored during the first thirteen years of my life.

I suppose, in considering soccer-related violence, our conversation illustrates two main points.

Firstly, that throwing your father into a nursing home because he can't remember anything about football in the seventies is, frankly, unfair. If he took you to any games he was probably far too busy looking after your precious hide to have noticed the scintillating back heel by a boyhood hero that still burns so brightly in your mind. Though it's hard to imagine - as he sits there in his truss and slippers talking nonsense - once upon a time, in an atmosphere of intense intimidation, Papa showed grace under pressure. Secondly, that if you have the misfortune to encounter stadium violence in the nineties, bearing in mind the most likely assault is a kick in the stomach from a half-time hot dog, don't worry about the long-term effects on your child.

Childhood is a time of tunnel vision, of living without fears or responsibilities. Then, more than at any other period in your life, the game really is all that matters. In twenty years time James Eager's Dad will remember the worry and the responsibility of that night in Dublin as though it were yesterday.

James will probably remember England being overrun and a David Kelly goal in the twenty-fifth minute.

School Football

Pamela Gillilan

My pal and I took on the catering,
Saturday mornings, we'd ride from Finchley
to Holloway's cut-price shops and stalls
in search of biscuits, spending pence
on the tram fare for a marginal saving.

The cheapest, whether arrowroot, Nice or tiffin,
or custard or orange creams sandwiching
sweet pastes of fiercely citrus colours,
all had the same texture, brittle and yet
too firm to melt in the mouth;
but the teams weren't connoisseurs -
after the match they piled into the pavilion
and rapidly wolfed down every crumb.
We lined up ready-poured cups of tea
and joked through the steam like amateur barmaids.

Our Saturdays' volunteering, though, led nowhere;
they'd troop off lugging their mud-stiff gear
towards their mothers' proper teas
while she and I wiped the counters,
washed the cups, counted the coppers.

Full time

Ken Elkes

The mourners gathered round the grave as Linda dabbed at her eyes with a screwed up piece of tissue.

She looked up at the naked trees at the edge of the graveyard, scratching the slate-coloured sky with their branches.

"This is all your fault," she thought, looking back down at her husband's coffin as the vicar's voice rose and fell with unfamiliar words.

"You and your bloody football. 39 years old and you still thought you were destined for greatness."

There right in front of her eyes was the blue and white flag he took to home games, now draped forlornly over the coffin lid.

John had, quite simply, been football mad. He took an almost childlike glee in reeling off facts and figures, even down to gate receipts for a 1964 Rovers FA cup fixture. It didn't matter where he was, football was always in his head. He would even clamour for the result of the Autoglass Trophy like it was the final of the World Cup.

"It keeps me out of the house, out of your way," he used to say on Saturdays as he pulled a number 9 shirt over his thermal vest.

On Sundays, when he would play for the Black Swan's second XI , his line was: "I've only got a few more seasons left in me. Can't you see we've got the rest of our lives to spend Sunday lunch together." Well, he was certainly wrong about that, thought Linda.

For years they had been involved in a war of attrition about a game which she could not understand. His enthusiasm for what he called the beautiful game was almost obsessive. But Linda had to admit at times she would get carried away herself as he talked about the game. She remembered the time he cowered behind the sofa during England's penalty shoot-out with Germany in the 1990 World Cup Finals.

"What's happening?" he bleated.

"Well, if you got off your knees and had a look you could see for yourself," she replied, sensing her own excitement at the drama on the screen.

"I can't, it's too much."

"Well, it's too late now, England have lost, that last bloke blasted it over the top of the goal."

He had stood up then, clutching a cushion as tears began to course down his face. "Never mind lads, you've done us proud, " he said to the television.

"They can't hear you, fool," said Linda.

"Oh they can ... in their hearts they can. That's why football is the greatest game men will ever play. It's an ecstasy and exquisite agony all in one," he said quietly, seriously.

At that moment she had felt a strange wonder at her husband and the agony on the faces of the players as they squatted, defeated, on the pitch. But deep inside her she knew she would never really understand why grown men developed a child-like wonder at running around in the rain kicking a soggy ball at each other. She would often tell him so, usually

right in the middle of a televised match on one of the satellite channels.

"What IS the point of this game," she would say, deliberately goading him, desperate for his attention.

"You know fine well what the point is, GO ON MY SON SHOOT. Oh my God you donkey, what was that?"

She tried a different tack: "Do you remember when we used to have a life together. When we did things on the spur of the moment, a couple of days away in Paris actually occurred back in the mists of time I seem to recall ..."

"Look sweetheart, if a couple of days away is what you want then organise it and I'll gladly go along. As long as it doesn't clash with any home games ... Come on referee let the game flow."

"The point I was trying to make is that I want you to treat me, do it for me," she said, exasperated.

"Okay, you organise it and I'll pay for it."

"Never mind."

They did go to Paris eventually. The first day was quite fun, but on the second day, after she had been out round the flea markets she came home to find John in front of the television watching highlights from the French second division.

And so it went on. The sniping and arguing occasionally resulting in a full blown row that simmered for days. Eventually one of them would break the silence, but things always returned to the same old routine.

"Well," thought Linda as she threw a handful of soil into the grave, "At least we managed to do something together on a Saturday at last."

Walking back to the car Linda remembered the night John died. He had gone downstairs and not returned. A couple of hours later she got up and found him on the kitchen floor. Massive coronary, the doctor said.

Even after he had gone, the habit was still there. Expecting him to walk through the door, leave his newspaper on the bathroom floor, switch on the football.

Habit, she thought. Is that what our love becomes, habit? Linda had been struck by how unmoved she had been by the death of a man she had lived with for the best part of 20 years. It was as if they had become caricatures for each other, just two dimensional people who happened to be married but never really got to know each other.

People at the wake noticed she had not cried once. She had not done since the death, they whispered. Instead she felt resigned, not even numb. Yet in the weeks that followed his funeral she found herself almost wanting him to come through the door after Rovers had suffered a 3-0 drubbing by some Northern mill town, just so she could take the piss.

She missed the banter. "So you're relegation hopefuls again this season are you?" she would have goaded him.

"Careful now woman. I may have lost a yard of pace but I could still reach you," he would have replied, only half joking.

When Linda felt ready, she went up into what had been their bedroom, closed the door and taking a deep breath, opened his wardrobe.

Curiously, she felt a calm detachment as she carefully folded his clothes into plastic bags ready for the charity shop. Nothing seemed familiar. They were just clothes, smelling not of John but of washing powder and conditioner. Even his soccer kit seemed strangely alien, as if someone else had just dropped it into her house.

At the bottom of the wardrobe were his football boots. Linda was just about to toss them into another bin liner when she hesitated. Carefully she pulled the boots out and the strong smell of earth, crushed grass and leather hit her.

At last the tears came pouring from her eyes. She sat and stared at the boots, following the curves and a tiny network of cracks and scars.

All those years she had known those feet, tickled them in bed as a prelude to sex, danced around them during days of courtship and once washed them after he came home from a match with a swollen, painful ankle. But she would never see them again.

Those boots were a strange contradiction. Showing the perfect outline of toe joint, little toe, heel and instep. Yet they were also a part of him that she had never reached, never able to comprehend his love of football. Now they were empty, the hole at the top gaping like a raw, hungry mouth.

Linda slid her hand down inside the boots trying to fill them, feeling the hard toes and harshness of the studs beneath her palm.

"Oh John, " she said out loud. "You old fool, why have you gone and left me."
In the end Linda decided to keep the boots, a bitter sweet symbol of their life together and apart.

A few days later she got a call from Terry, John's best man and fellow stalwart of the Black Swan team.

"Hello Linda, you all right? Listen. I was wondering, it's your birthday next Saturday and well I thought you might want to come along to a game, you know, down at Rovers. It's just an idea, perhaps not a very good one on second thoughts."

"No Terry, I think it's a great idea. Maybe it's about time I found out what all the fuss has been about," replied Linda with a smile.

Worshipping at the Church of the Ciderhead

Ross Burnham

Why do I support Bristol City? What strange force took me to Ashton Gate to watch these sometimes particularly untalented eleven men kicking a ball? And how has that strange force kept me turning up again and again, rain and shine?

I grew up in a family that had no interest in football. My older brother was more interested in Lambrettas and the Stones, and my sister, in Cliff Richard. I guess the first stirrings must have occurred at Junior School when I started to kick a ball around. The game seemed fun and a way of making everyone equal - that is, unless you were one of the fat kids who hung around the goal talking about how many Aztec bars you could buy for your half-a-crown pocket money. I also seemed to be half decent at kicking this thing about, although my skills were measured by the fact that I had a prodigious toe-punt which enabled me to kick a ball further than the others but unfortunately not in any particular direction. For one of the smallest kids this was looked upon as quite a feat by the other budding George Bests and Peter Osgoods in the class.

After a while I was picked to play for the school team. The rest of the class had taken off to the Swimming Pool on the usual weekly lesson, leaving myself and one other kid behind to get on with some crappy work that we had been set. Unknown to me at the time, the whole class chose that week to re-enact Pearl Harbour in the local baths, and what did our teacher do? He banned them all from playing football later that week leaving just me and the other guy to play a pretty lame game of three and in. Also unknown to me was the fact that the games teacher was watching our efforts from the main building, and was impressed by my left footed projectile efforts, again, inaccurate but lengthy.

A perk of being picked for the team was the opportunity to purchase the odd ticket to attend Bristol Boys representative games, and to attend the occasional England Boys match at Wembley, yelling abuse at eleven poor Dutch schoolboys. The latter usually took place around FA Cup Semi-Final time and this enabled me to have a go at buying two rosettes that would hopefully represent the finalists. My dad usually made the choice (knowing little about football) and he managed to select the losers nearly every time. If only this had been later in the seventies/eighties I could have persuaded him to pick Liverpool a few times and stop the bastards from winning everything in sight. And they put their successes down to Shankly, Paisley and Co - little did they know it was my old man.

Another boy in my class went on to achieve success in the game even though I could kick the damn thing further than he could. His name was, and still is, Gary Mabbutt, and he went on to play for the dreaded enemy Trumpton Rovers - The Gas! Anyway, back to the subject, why did I choose Bristol City? Well, having marvelled at the 1970 World Cup Finals, and also having taken a liking to Chelsea (it was either that or Leeds if you were a small boy at that time, and artistry should always defeat out and out thuggery) I decided to ask my Dad to take me to a 'proper' game. I had a choice of either Bristol City or the unmentionables. Fate took a hand and for no particular reason I headed to see the boys in red. Brazil and Bristol City, the chasm didn't seem to be yawning so much when you're ten.

For my eleventh birthday Dad and I turned up at Ashton Gate to see Preston North End take on what instantly became 'my team'. I hadn't realised until looking up the date today out of interest, that it was April 1st 1972,

rather prophetic. We purchased a programme for the princely sum of 5p - little did I know that this would become an all-consuming hobby in my teens - no, I didn't have an anorak, and took our places in the ground in the new-ish Dolman Stand. My Dad also bought me a hat, a vinyl cap that made you sweat like a fiddler's armpit, possibly the cause of my impending baldness 22 years later, and a rosette. I was already floating away on the heady whiff of woodbines and stale urine, and the wonderful language that was emanating from a couple of guys near us. You didn't get professional swearing like this at Junior School!

When the City team was announced I was astounded when one particular player's name drew an even greater level of colourfully violent language from the crowd - what could this poor chap have done to deserve this treatment? Twenty three years later, this question has been answered a thousand times over as my mates and I have questioned the parental status of many a player to have worn the red and white. As the game unfolded I looked at the Preston team's photo in the programme, and read the Pen Pictures as they were called then, not Player Profiles etc, and the manager had notes rather than a column which always sounded like it had sexual connotations. I asked my dad where Preston was and he told me it was "up north". I reckoned this meant they would be rougher, bigger, and from a poorer background than us, what a snob, and I was already taking a severe disliking to them. I can remember some of their players now - Keely, Spavin, Ricky Heppolette ...

On our side the number ten took my eye - he was young, skilful, long-haired and seemed like our own version of George Best. His name? Gerry Gow, later of Manchester City, a player who would display the skills loved by all fans - a tackle like steel, a complete disregard for anyone's safety (let alone his own), and a definite leaning towards GBH. I can't imagine what hero worship he would gain from the lads on the terraces today. In fact, whenever I see a video of Ricky Villa's wonderful goal in the FA Cup Final against Spurs I marvel at the fact that at the beginning of his mazy dribble my hero decided not to put in a bone-crunching tackle that would have put the said Argie in hospital and thus re-written the football history books.

Well the reds did me proud on my birthday and stuffed the men from up north 4-1. I was hooked, and the feelings of pride - and vinyl sweatiness - when I wore my hat and rosette to school on Monday were immeasurable. If I had had any sort of chest at that age, I'm sure it would have bust a few buttons. From that day on City were my team. I migrated to the terraces (It was expensive if you went regularly, and the terraces looked far better fun, sitting on the wall at the front, so near that you occasionally got splashed with a bit of your hero's sweat, or even blood. My old man kept going for a while, but I reckoned he only went for a smoke of his pipe, banned from the house by my Mum).

I now had a bonding with thousands of others, something that would make me instant friends in years to come, and would also save me money. A guy who serviced an old car of mine supported City and he used to knock a few quid off. Forget the thousands that I must have spent following them over the years. I've also turned down dates - one, anyway - knocked off school, and visited numerous inhospitable places just to see the reds. To my delight I've also been able to convert others to the Church of the Ciderhead. What times I've had. Promotion to the First Division (the proper First Division mind you - not the one we've just plummeted out of), the last gasp survival against Coventry - the only decent thing that knobhead Jimmy Hill's ever done - two trips to Wembley, the Littlewoods Semi-Final against Notts Forest, the FA Cup wins against Chelsea and Liverpool, the climb back from Division Four, and best of all - beating the Gas. It's irrational, it's insane, but it's been brilliant. What else would I have done with all those Saturday afternoons?

Haiku

Pamela Gillilan

Match of the Day. Years
of it unwatched in this house
since your last winter

Me Against the Multitude

Bob Turvey

Dad was a Villa supporter because he lived in Birmingham. The season he was eight the Villa scored 128 goals, which is still the record for the First Division. It wasn't always unalloyed joy though. He was twelve and a half on December 14 1935. That was the day the mighty Arsenal visited. As he told it, Ted Drake, the Arsenal centre forward, only touched the ball eight times. Seven times it ended in the back of the net, and once it hit the crossbar. It still stands as the record for individual goals in a First Division match. The Villa lost 7-1. Worse was to come; they got relegated that season.

We moved to Marple Bridge when I was eight. Nobody ever knows where that is, but when you say it's a pretty village near Stockport, which is near Manchester, most people have an idea. At the local primary school all the boys supported Manchester City or Manchester United. Except me. There was no real problem. United were probably playing their best football ever; even I knew that. The Busby Babes were outstanding. In 1957 they won the league. They had also reached the Cup Final, and if they won the cup they would become only the third side ever to have achieved the double. The last side who won the double was way back in 1897 - a team from Birmingham called Aston Villa. And by one of those remarkable coincidences which nature and sport throw up when you least expect them, the side they were playing at Wembley was a team from Birmingham called Aston Villa. To say tension was high at school would be an understatement. I was nearly ten; everyone else, even the City fans, wanted United to win the cup and to show that the double could be achieved. Pundits at the time believed that it couldn't, because they felt that the pressures of the game had become much more intense since the last century. It was said that it would take an exceptional team to win the double; a team like no other; a team of footballing geniuses. A team, in fact, like Manchester United.

Everyone kept telling me that United would crucify the Villa. I was told to have my handkerchief ready. At home, even Dad said it would be a difficult match. Everyone knew that Manchester United would win. Looking back, with hindsight, everyone was right. United were the best team in Europe, possibly the world. At the time I didn't see it like that. Villa were my team, and they had to win.

My mother tells me that I watched the match on our television fully kitted out in my Villa colours. Claret and the bobble hat, scarf, rattle. All home made of course, including the rattle. You couldn't buy Villa colours in Manchester. I only remember one incident from the match. Peter McParland shoulder charged Ray Wood, the United goalie. They were both concussed. Wood suffered a broken cheek and was stretchered off. United played with ten men. McParland scored two goals. United could only manage one. Things would of course have been different had the modern rules about shoulder charging the goalkeeper been in force. But they weren't. The goalkeeper was fair game. Things would of course have been different if substitutions were allowed. But they weren't. So the Villa won. They took the cup back to Birmingham, and the pundits in the Sunday papers all said that it was unlikely that the double would ever be won again, if a team as great as the Busby Babes couldn't do it. And the pundits in the Sunday papers said it was a great pity that the McParland incident had occurred. There was a lot of discussion about the physical nature of football. Most unbiased people seemed to agree. Even my mother, who had watched the match in between cooking Saturday dinner had been heard to comment that McParland was a dirty fouler and shouldn't be allowed on the pitch.

With hindsight, and being an adult now, I agree. It was a dirty foul. And United should probably have won the Cup.

But they didn't. And I wasn't an adult at the time. And my team won. And I went into school on Monday, and I told everyone that fact. Because it was a fact. The Villa won the Cup. I felt wonderful.

First time

Jim McNeill

first time I went to see middlesbrough
play i was about ten
they were playing charlton
athletic at home
an when the reds scored i thought
at last its time for
the uninhibited use of my
new heavy voice
a kids roar
i was lost in it
all jumping up an down
gainst concete terrace
an barrier
till i noticed my fathers thickening shadow
an i heard him speak of the change of strip
an that i should be cheering
for the losing side

More than a Game

Elliot Feltham

"Football is more than a game." A cliché
maybe, but nevertheless true. Football is not a
game, it's a way of life. A life that is not quite
normal, which begins in August
and ends the following May, except every two
years when the summer is filled with either the
European Nations' Cup or the World Cup.

There are many people who are
'footballholics'. It is a painful addiction where
sufferers can be found on balmy summer
evenings watching children kicking tennis balls
between coats placed on the floor acting as
goal posts. They will watch anything for their
kicks. Even video highlights of Bristol Rovers.

I am one of this breed. A Bristol City
season ticket holder since the age of ten and a
well worn away traveller. I have never once
enjoyed a match. How can you when your
whole happiness depends on the outcome, an
outcome that is totally out of your control no
matter how many lucky shirts, jumpers,
cigarettes etc that you care to bring to the
game?

My whole life is mirrored by BCFC.
Meaningless and totally useless dates - the sort
which normal people forget - I remember, but
only through the parallel with the City. I have
no recollection of anything between June and
July, but for the rest of my time my mind is
brimming with innumerable facts and trivia.

The day I finished with a childhood
sweetheart for the lure of an older woman? -
A pathetically inept 1-0 defeat at Torquay.

The day I passed my driving test? - It was the
day before we drew 2-2 at Mansfield.

The day I met the woman who was to
become my wife? - May 5 1990, we beat
Walsall 4-0 and won promotion. I knew she
was destined to become my wife when I
mentioned to her that the God Mark Gavin
had scored, and she replied that only that
morning she'd cut his hair! A dream date if
ever there was one.

My wife gets on very well with my parents,
but if there was one thing for which she could

resent my Dad, it was he who was responsible for my 'addiction'.

He took me to my first game. It was in the late seventies against Bristol Rovers in the Gloucester Cup Final, which we won 4-0. My ecstasy was short lived when my Dad told me that we were the only two teams in the competition.

I got my first season ticket in 1980. The club had just been relegated to the Second Division, but I didn't care. I was finally going to get to go to the Mecca, not just occasionally, but every other week. Looking back, the team were awful, but I was just glad to be there. The envy of my school friends.

The club was relegated that season, and then the next. After four months of the next season they were bottom of the whole league. I was beginning to think it was me. In three years I'd seen them win 15 times. I was never sad, it just didn't matter. I was too young for disappointment. But my Dad used to swear a lot.

Then something happened. They started winning games. So this was what it was like. Who needed girls when there was Glyn Riley? I was well and truly hooked. On one occasion the *Evening Post* carried a photograph of Jon Economou scoring against Hartlepool. In the background was an empty Grandstand, apart from me and my Dad. The framed photo is still on my wall now.

The next few seasons were fantastic. Two Wembley visits, missing promotion by a couple of points, play-offs, Nottingham Forest in the Littlewoods Cup Semi, and then ultimately that promotion in 1990, mainly thanks to Joe Jordan, Bob Taylor and Mark Gavin. Then Jordan left, Taylor left and Gavin left, came back, and left again. Jimmy Lumsden was sacked, Denis Smith bought Andy Cole, saved us from being relegated, and was sacked. The team was rubbish. Dull and boring. It became so bad that I even stopped watching Match of the Day. Football depressed me.

Joe Jordan returned but it was too late. For the first time I really felt dejected. The disappointment of relegation was huge. Those before didn't count. Now I know why my Dad swore so much. I almost began to hate the club. But against Reading during the last home game of the season something changed. Watching the massed ranks of away supporters celebrate, I remembered when that was me, and I knew that we'd be back.

Everything slotted into place. My Dad still sat next to me, we still had Joe Jordan, and there's always next year.

Playing the Long Bore Game

Melissa Feltham

Question: How many women know anything about football?
Answer: Not many. It is an exclusive club for men who talk about it in riddles.

- It's a game of two halves.

- Players can hang in the air.

- He didn't get enough purchase on the ball.

- Goalkeepers can narrow the angle.

- Small players have a low centre of gravity.

- They've set their stall out.

- Players can turn on a sixpence.

Does anyone understand what all this means? It would appear that football players are shopkeepers, mathematicians and ballet dancers. This probably isn't too far from the truth. Reading the daily sleaze papers, football seems to be full of money-mad, gambling prima-donnas.

I'm sorry. Try as hard as I might, I just can't see what the attraction is. It is always cold, I can never see, the team my husband supports always lose, and please can anybody explain to me how this offside thing works?

Bottoming Out

Paul Vezey

My team, Bristol City, have never been among the more successful football clubs to grace the game and the team that I recall with most affection was the worst in its trophy-starved history.

The season was 1982/83 during which City had the distinction of occupying bottom place of the Football League and attracting their lowest average attendance this century, about 4,500 fans. But it was more significant to me because during that season my obsession for the club became cemented.

During the previous season the club's future had been in doubt following its 'freefall' through the League from its heady days in Division One. Financial problems had culminated in the club being within hours of going out of existence. It was a time of great personal turmoil. The integral structure of my life could have been taken from me. If the club folded, what would I do with my Saturday afternoons? Supporting any other side would not have worked as I would have continued to think back to my first love.

Having experienced this, it was with great relief and optimism that I travelled to Ashton Gate to see City start the 82/83 season in Division Four. The club had been left with a handful of hardened professionals and several willing youngsters. One major addition was the appointment of Terry Cooper as player manager. Honest, open and accessible to the supporters, his enthusiasm and commitment to the team were inspirational. I can still visualise him moving with his legs appearing permanently bent at the knees, barrel chested and hunched. He had graced the greatest stages of the game. Now he was dragging his tired limbs over Gresty Road, The Shay and The Recreation Ground, but still with great effect.

By the end of September my optimism had

been shattered once again, four goals conceded at Crewe and seven at Northampton leaving the team in the bottom four of the Football League.

Despite the team's ongoing failings the four thousand supporters who stayed loyal to the cause never wavered. The supporters who remained were those who would always remain, it was the most positive backing that I had experienced in my years of following the Club. This was the first City team for many seasons that contained several locally born players. We could identify with this team, it truly represented Bristol. We empathised with the young players thrown into the most unsuccessful side in the League. The players were encouraged, cajoled and consoled.

The playing style was one of reckless attacking abandon, totally unlike previous City teams that I had witnessed. Matches were entertaining, the play naive and punctuated by crass mistakes that would hand the points to the opposition.

At the end of October, unbeaten leaders Wimbledon visited Ashton Gate. The 'Dons' were at the 'lift-off' stage of their rapid ascent through the divisions. Already apparent was the direct, over-physical approach that was to make them loathed over subsequent seasons. City, second from bottom of the League having lost six out of ten League games, were expected to extend their dismal run of results.

For the first time in months everything connected in the team's play, they hit Wimbledon with a hurricane-force display of attacking football. I could see the cumbersome 'Dons' defenders' over-confidence visibly drain before my eyes, as the nimble City forwards ran repeatedly at them. By half-time City had scored three goals - one most memorably, when tiny Jon Economou left three Wimbledon players in his wake on a mazy run through the penalty area. Just when it looked as though he had lost his opportunity, he casually chipped the ball across from the dead-ball line into the head of a grateful Alan Nicholls who couldn't miss from three yards out. The crowd were euphoric, all the frustrations and tribulations of the previous three seasons were released. WHOAHH! YEAHHH!

In the second half, Wimbledon managed to regain their composure but the damage was already done. Glyn Riley managed to obtain his third goal, becoming the first City player to score a 'hat-trick' for four years and City had won 4-2.

Victory did not signify an immediate reversal in the team's fortunes. Four draws and two defeats resulted in City completing their descent to the basement of the Football League by December. Hitting rock bottom in such record-breaking time came as a relief. There was only one way for City to go now.

Around this time Forbes Phillipson-Masters was introduced to the team. A cultured name he may have had, but a cultured centre-half he was not. Big, clumsy, a deadringer for Chevy Chase, but he brought defensive organisation where before had been chaos. Never one to play the ball out of defence, he would prefer to hoof the ball upfield or into the enclosure. His presence and the fact that the team were becoming more accustomed to each other led to a gradual improvement in results through January and February. In March, the team started an unbeaten nine match run. By the season's end, City had reached fourteenth position and were displaying signs of becoming the promotion challengers that they became the following year.

The last home match of the season, against Crewe, was witnessed by 4,700 spectators. At the final whistle, City winning 2-1, the crowd ran on to the pitch in celebration, as if the championship had been won. I remember Terry Cooper leading the team on a lap of honour carrying a banner with the message THANK YOU FOR YOUR SUPPORT.

It had been a season when players and supporters had been totally united. I have not known a season like it before, or during more successful times since. Bristol City were alive and kicking, they were on the way back.

Watching the team on their lap of honour, I felt proud, emotional and satisfied. I was glad to still be a supporter of Bristol City FC.

Meeting a Hero

Simon Fry

Meeting your heroes is a calculated risk. Somebody honoured and worshipped from afar has little scope to disappoint. The fan filters out the negative and cocoons his hero in an aura where he can do no wrong. It is only when this image is made flesh that mystique may be tarnished.

In December 1994, Villa Park staged a memorial match for the dependents of Tony Barton. Tony Barton is the only man to have managed Aston Villa to the highest honour in European club football, the European Champions' Cup, which they won in 1982.

Between 1974 and 1982, however, Ron Saunders managed the club. He had brought the League Championship to the Villa for the first time in seventy one years in 1981. His planning, guidance and vision transformed Aston Villa from Division Two also-rans to the finest team in Europe in eight seasons. This was in the days when success in football depended on such qualities rather more than a backer's millions.

And what a team he formed! In the victorious 1980/81 season only 14 players were used. A buccaneer spirit ran through the club as this band won their prize in style. The grace of Gordon Cowans. Tony Marlowe's spellbinding wing play. Allan Evans and Ken McNaught - they shall not pass. Peter Withe's fervour. Led by the superlative Dennis Mortimer, the team had huge self-belief without a hint of arrogance.

While his team swept all aside - seven wins in a row in early 1981 - Saunders remained a confusing figure. His team played with panache and flair, comparable to any team of its day. Saunders, however, was seen as dour and glum, little given to the demands of the media.

The media needs people to talk about. Aston Villa were a team with no players of household name status. Saunders then would be the focus. Not renowned for his charisma, he didn't take kindly to being asked to smile, like some taciturn child. That his players did the talking for him - and how - seems to have been missed.

Living in Bristol, away from the Midlands, this was the impression I had of Ron Saunders. One built by label-pinners.

At the 1981 Charity Shield match I sang his name to 'Amazing Grace'. He wore his popularity with humility and not a little disbelief as we thanked him to the tune of a hymn, for bringing us to the Promised Land.

I can remember where I was when I heard that he had left the club, in February 1982.

So on that wintry night in December 1994, I travelled to Villa Park. Ron was to nominally manage the team he'd built 15 years earlier - in a friendly against other veterans. The chance to see the great man, from however far away, for possibly the last time could not be missed.

Buying the more expensive upper tier seats, I would be unable to get to pitch level. When explaining my wish to meet Ron to one of the club's notoriously Jobsworth officials, I was refused access to the pitch. I returned to my seat with tears not far away.

The match that followed the friendly compounded my sadness. Yet another of the subsequent poor shadows of Villa teams demonstrated the mediocrity that has been so largely characteristic since the halcyon early 1980s.

And then I glanced down to the Directors' Box. A sturdy, bald man was talking away to a fairly elderly lady. It somehow seemed obvious that neither knew the other, yet they chattered with genuine warmth and mutual interest. Part of me knew this was Ron, but part of me refused to believe it.

For five minutes I kept looking down, needing to know, but scared of being proved wrong. If this was Ron Saunders, I might never get another chance to speak to him again.

Eventually the lady returned to her seat, and I instantly approached the box. Looking over the small partition, I met Ron and he smiled.

I asked him to sign my autograph book and we talked of the day and his emotions - Ron had first met Tony in the Portsmouth team of the early 1960s. I felt so privileged to thank Ron for his service to the club that much of our meeting simply passed me by.

My abiding memory, though, is of a delightful girl, with huge curly locks of hair, clinging to Ron throughout our conversation. The night was cold and she held on to him as though holding on to a lifebelt at sea. She looked up and waited patiently as Ron met the people for whom he means so much.

When asked what he does with his time now he smiled and talked of the golf course, and of spending time with his grandchildren, nodding down to the infant at his side. He squeezed her lovingly, and the image of Ron Saunders, morose and stolid, lifted like a veil.

In memory of my brother, Andy, who first took me to the Villa.

Anfield Dream

Jeff Bolitho

This is Anfield. This legendary, imposing welcome to visiting teams is sufficient to make grown men quiver in their boots. And tonight, February 11th 1992, the legend that is Liverpool Football Club was to host an FA Cup replay against the team I have followed since I was four years old - Bristol Rovers.

Anfield was everything I had expected, and more. I was entranced by the splendid turf, the Kemlyn Road Stand, and particularly the Kop, before finding my seat. The night proved to be quite an occasion. Liverpool had won the right to a replay the previous week after a thrilling 1-1 at Twerton, though the travelling masses at Anfield were not convinced. "Lucky, lucky Liverpool," rang out the cry amongst 7,000 blue-and-white Bristolians before kick off. Surely, when the team saw this fantastic support their nerves would subside a little. After all, Liverpool are going through their period of reconstruction back to greatness aren't they? Well, that may have been the case during the ill-fated Souness reign, but any team which steps out in the world-famous stadium and gazes into a packed Kop in full cry, cannot fail to be awe-struck and, I daresay, rather intimidated.

So, on with the match. It was not long before the anthem of "Goodnight Irene" echoed around the ground. Scousers asked each other "Who's this Irene?" "Is that their manager?" and "What number is she playing then?" This seemed to inspire the morale of the troops, who surged forward insolently, in cheeky defiance of reputations. They aren't allowed to do this at Anfield, are they?

Then, the footballing public around the country heard the inevitable on the radio - Saunders had scored. Hold on though - shouldn't that be Dean Saunders, Liverpool's Welsh international? Nope. Carl "Billy Ocean" Saunders scored one of the most sensational strikes I have ever seen by a Rovers player. He even had the audacity to score it in front of a stunned Kop. Were the mighty Reds on their way out ? A mixture of wild celebration and delirium broke out at the other end of the ground. "There's only one Billy Ocean," acclaimed the ecstatic Gasheads.

Liverpool have a reputation for only reaching top gear in the second half. Lull the opposition into a false sense of security - toy with them, even - and then strike. Unfortunately for us, tonight was no exception. The Red Machine came out roaring in the second half, inspired by the supreme dribbling skills of Steve Mcmanaman. Another myth was also about to be put to the test - could the Kop really "suck in" a goal? This has to be nonsense. Not so. The Koppites seem to magically sense a goal, and raise the noise level accordingly at such a time. Having been out-sung in the first half by the Rovers fans, the cries urging Liverpool onward were now truly deafening. Before long we were jolted back to grim reality - 2-1 down. Well, it was only a dream, wasn't it?

Football Crazy

Asif Hussaini

I like football because it is fast and furious. It is great fun taking shots and scoring goals. In football you have to have confidence that you will win otherwise you may lose.

If you're a goalie keep an eye on the ball. If an opponent is coming run out and tackle him. If you're a defender when the ball comes get it and kick it to a mid-fielder. If you're a mid-fielder when you have the ball dribble it and when an opponent comes kick it to a striker. If you're a striker try to set up goals. You never know what could happen!

My best players are Roberto Baggio of Italy and Romario of Brazil. I watched the whole of the World Cup 1994. Brazil won but all the teams did well.

I play football every day in school and usually my team wins. I am one of the best players in my class. I couldn't believe that Manchester United lost to Everton in the FA Cup Final. I don't go to a club but I am playing a 5-a-side Constables Cup tournament in my school. I think that my school will win the cup.

In training sessions first you should get another person and start getting in positions and start passing to each other. Then spread out and start passing. Then start to dribble a ball. Learn to keep control of the ball. Next tell someone to try and get past you with the ball. Keep on trying to get the ball. If you do it 5 times then you have mastered tackling. Next, try to make tactics of your own. Then tell someone to get in goal and take shots at them from different places.

If you want to be excellent at football try and play as much as you can. Even if you have not played football before you could become a football superstar, or even become football crazy!

Home-Grown Football

H. D. Bevan

This is the place to show off the latest Bristol City strip where it will be properly appreciated. The times I come home from work to find a note saying, "Up Hillside".

Two words but such a wealth of meanings: expect him when I see him. His homework isn't done - again. He will be dirty, bruised, and possibly bleeding. He will insist on giving me a blow by blow account of the game.

"Hillside" is the estate next door. It has a five-a-side pitch with Astroturf. The kids organise games among themselves. Fixtures are announced by a boy on a bike at the back door with words like, "You're needed, they've got eight we only got six." What boy would not respond to such a battle cry?

It can be five-a-side, six-a-side, or whoever turns up. The game lasts for three hours plus injury time, extra time, and ends in a penalty shoot-out. The score can reach phenomenal proportions, in the region sixteen to fourteen, and they are counting - carefully!

The ball they use is not really ancient, it's

just had a hard life. Half the leather is missing, and it needs pumping up every game. It must have belonged to one of them at some time, but now it goes home with whoever is the last to leave. So it's no good hoping that the game will stop when the boy who owns the ball goes home for tea.

The referee is whoever is the strongest. A foul gets a thump, a bad foul means a short fight, and the game goes on.

Although the contest is between "Woodside" and "Hillside", to the uninitiated it might seem that it's Bristol City versus Bristol City. Other teams are occasionally represented but the Bristol City strip is seen at every turn.

Do you remember those plain red "Robin" tops, and the equally plain yellow "away" strip, when "Hire Rite" were the sponsors? The "Thorn Security" yellow and green "away" strip looks less bilious now in its faded glory. Still worn with the yellow socks, albeit by a younger brother. And the vibrant purple and green, with white and purple socks. Sadly the socks have not fared so well in the wash, but Mother discards them at her peril.

The red "Auto Windscreen" strip doesn't seem so interesting somehow as the "Dry Blackthorn", with its background of black shading (which used to mask the stains that would not come out). Parts of the strip can always be seen, even if not in the combinations visualised by the designers.

Still, when all is said and done, at least I know where he is, who he's with, what he's doing, and he's happy. What is more, we all know what to give him for his birthday.

Journey to Highbury

Elaine Amos

I was completely ignorant about football until the 1961 Cup Final between Tottenham Hotspur and Leicester City. The year of the 'Double', and the year I discovered my first ever hero, Danny Blanchflower. I can remember the match on TV as if it was yesterday, with Kenneth Wolstenholme's dulcet tones announcing the names of the greatest team of the era: Brown, Baker, Henry, Blanchflower, Norman, Mackay, Jones, White, Smith, Dyson, Allen.

Spurs had won the League Championship the week before, and were now bidding to become the first team of the century to capture the elusive League and Cup Double. They duly beat Leicester 2-0, and my new hero held the Cup high, in front of thousands of adoring fans, his place in history guaranteed. From that moment, I was totally hooked.

I became a keen collector of photographs of my hero. My Mum took me to stay with my aunt and uncle in Plaistow every Easter, and my aunt bought me the special Cup Final edition of *Charles Buchan's Football Monthly*, with the victorious Spurs team plastered all over the front cover. Unfortunately for me, Plaistow was deep in West Ham territory, and my uncle was an avid supporter. No amount of persuasion would make him take me to White

Hart Lane. It was the Hammers or nothing, so off I went with him to Upton Park, to see Moore, Peters, Hurst and the rest. My heart still belonged to Spurs, however. My Mum took me to see *South Pacific*, and I remember coming out of the subway of Tottenham Court Road tube station, and looking everywhere for the White Hart Lane floodlights. Sad, isn't it?

The following year, my Dad - on leave from the Merchant Navy - took me to my first match at Ashton Gate, an FA Cup 1st round tie against Wellington Town. I can remember nothing of the match, only the record 'Bobby's Girl', by Susan Maughan.

Isn't it amazing how songs bring back memories? We went to the next round tie too, against Wimbledon, then a Southern League club. Throughout the 1960s, whenever Dad was on leave, we would go to either City or Rovers. I remember the old wooden stand at Eastville, 7/6d to get in, and an old codger calling out "rubbish Brown" at regular intervals to the hapless John Brown.

My love affair with Spurs had abated with Danny Blanchflower's retirement, in 1964. I now had a pen friend in Blackpool called Lorraine, who lived near my cousins, where Mum and I used to stay during the summer holidays. Lorraine supported Blackpool - then a First Division club - and I went with her to Bloomfield Road on a number of occasions. She had a kid brother who allowed her to join in kick-abouts with his friends. Boy, was I envious. Throughout the season, Lorraine would send me programmes of the matches she had attended, so that started another

hobby, which I still continue.

One year, Blackpool were due to play Cardiff City, so we arranged to meet at Ninian Park station. This was the first time I had been on a longish train journey on my own. When I arrived at the station, there was not a football fan in sight, only a solitary ticket collector. We started talking and he revealed that he was a nephew of the great Charles Buchan! The Blackpool match was forgotten, but the afternoon not wasted.

Meanwhile, at school, I was looked upon as a bit of a freak. The 1960s may have been swinging, but not so revolutionary as to teach football to girls at a mixed comprehensive. It was hockey or nothing, chum!

I went off to college to study PE, and apart from a visit to Molineux to see Wolves take on Best, Charlton, Law and eight others, and to see Rodney at Loftus Road, my interest in football took a back seat to other activities available to students. My first teaching job was at Merrywood Girls' School, back in Bristol, and I did have the privilege of teaching Keith Fear's sister, Carol, a natural athlete. A lot of the girls tolerated my passion for football, and I was allowed to organise Staff v Pupil matches.

That year, I met John, my husband-to-be, in the guise of my driving instructor. He admitted to being a dormant Arsenal fan (go on, say it - aren't they all?). He also supports Gillingham, so we always went to watch them at Eastville or Ashton Gate, and also at Priestfield Stadium if we were staying in Kent.

My life changed in May 1989 when Arsenal went to Anfield needing to beat Liverpool by 2 clear goals to clinch the First Division championship. Nobody gave them a chance of course, and Liverpool were supremely confident. We watched the match on a portable TV in our caravan. When Arsenal scored their first goal, I became so engrossed that I came out with the most outrageous statement ever. "If Arsenal win, I promise to support them for evermore." Has anyone else said anything so outlandish? My husband looked at me in amazement, and checked the whisky bottle. Anyway, Michael Thomas duly obliged, and scored a magnificent goal in the 92nd minute. Arsenal were the champions, we danced around the caravan, and my fate was sealed. I had made a promise, and Thomas had made sure that I would have to keep it.

Sure enough, my indoctrination began in August of that year with a visit to Wembley to see the Gunners play Liverpool again, in the Charity Shield this time. A few weeks later I was taken to pay homage at Highbury, 'the Home of Football' (their words, not mine). I have to admit that I was completely bowled over by the sheer magnetism of the place. We go there, as and when finances allow, and when we can get in. We did manage to get on the north bank before it was converted into a stand, and found it not the least bit intimidating. I am a keen student of the history of the club, would you believe? Is there anyone else in Bristol who will admit to this infatuation?

Despite my new found adulation, John had a moment of weakness, and agreed to grant my old ambition to visit White Hart Lane. The match was Cyril Knowles' Memorial match, against Arsenal, who else? I tried to imagine Danny's boys on that pitch, but my heart was now lost to the marble halls of Highbury.

I am of course the butt of endless jokes from the City purists at work. The hilarity when I wore my Arsenal pullover on the day after Nayim's ridiculous goal in the Cup Winner's Cup had to be heard to be believed.

I don't care. We sleep in a bedroom dominated by a photograph of the 1989 champions over the bed, and a scarf draped over the mirror. A clock, lampshade and numerous books adorn the lounge. The brainwashing is complete.

Curious Brown Eyes - Bristol 4

Sandra Britton

'Fantasy Football' isn't a Nineties idea. I played it in 1956, when I was thirteen, when the Rovers beat the Busby Babes in the 3rd Round Cup match, when I worshipped Alfie Biggs' flowing blonde locks and Barrie Meyer's thighs. Until this day I've never seen a pair of legs to match his: not even the sculptured perfection of Michelangelo's *David* comes close. I was watching a cricket match with my son on TV last summer, when a portly, ageing umpire filled the screen. Oh Barrie! I wasn't watching whether you gave the batsmen out - I was rolling back the years trying to recapture the

delights that I knew were hidden under your long white coat.

Like many early-teenage girls my burgeoning sexuality found release in the hero worship of footballers. Thirteen is a time for 'firsts'. My first indecent assault happened on the terraces, although I didn't identify it as such at the time. Joy Hutchings and I, sporting blue and white scarves, rattles and bobble-hats used to get to Eastville hours before the game, so that we could get as near the pitch as possible. Only much later did I realise that, as Joy Hutchings and I were almost the only spectators in sight, there was actually no crowd pressure jamming the man in the raincoat against my back. That was all he did - that and heavy breathing. When I turned round to see who was pushing, he went red in the face with embarrassment and apologised. Even the crime was more innocent then ...

Joy Hutchings - I never knew why, but everyone always referred to her by her full name - lived in Duckmoor Road and being geographically inclined to the 'Robins', she had a serious conflict of loyalties. Although I was sensitive to her difficulties and occasionally deigned to grace Ashton Gate with my presence, she knew that being friends with me meant me and all the Pirates, and learning the words to "Goodnight Irene."

Although the term had yet to be coined, 'Feminism' and I first flirted in the shadow of the Gasworks. I wrote to Bert Tann in confrontational tone, demanding to be a 'ballboy' behind the goal. I could think of no greater excitement in the world than chasing Howard Radford's balls. Not surprisingly, Bert never replied.

During the last week in July, first in August, Joy Hutchings and I would make our annual pilgrimage to Uphill where our gladiators got into shape for the forthcoming season. I suppose today's equivalent of "going to Uphill" must be going to Florida. To be near them, to talk, to joke, to collect autographs, to bask in the reflected glow of celebrity ... Our futures which stretched before us down the years could hold no more intense a thrill - we knew that for sure. The days were long and hot, and what a team we had! Geoff Bradford, Dai Ward, Alfie Biggs ... Georgie Petherbridge on one wing and Peter Hooper on the other. I loved the way his surname translates into Bristolese as 'Upper' which only a true Bristolian can pronounce properly - and I still remember dear Harry Bamford whenever I go past the junction of Apsley Road and Blackboy Hill.

I used to boast that our family had a 'special relationship' with the Rovers, but the connection was a bit loose. The Baker family lived in Bellevue Road, Eastville and my Dad was on the turnstile on Saturday afternoons, eking out his meagre pay from the chocolate factory. Legend had it that he had actually been on the Rovers' books before the War, but as a challenging, cynical adolescent I didn't believe him.

One of his brothers was married to the sister of the person who ran the catering at Eastville and I was allowed to serve in the 'Buffee' at half-time with my Auntie Rene. This was a little white shack in the middle of the terraces, from whose hatch we brewed steaming, strong tea, dispensing it rapidly from wide-spouted teapots by rhythmic sloshing up and down rows of white china mugs. I can't remember what happened to Joy Hutchings when I moved into the Buffee. I think she went back to Ashton Gate.

I had brief flirtations with Bert Trautman, the goalie for Manchester City (Aryan, blue-eyed blonde), Albert Quigley (did he play for Doncaster? I can't remember, but I do remember that I went off him when I found out he took ballet lessons) and Alick Jefferies (black hair, smouldering eyes) whose career was cut short by a broken leg. But my enthusiasm was on the wane. Shortly after the Buffee, I lost interest in footballers completely and started spending Saturday afternoons getting ready for Saturday nights at The Glen or The Spa.

Do you remember the *Pink 'Un* and the *Green 'Un*? 'The Traveller' used to write a column dealing with readers' queries, so I wrote to ask him to find some details of my Dad's alleged signing. The answer was duly published, addressed to 'Dear Curious Brown Eyes, Bristol 4'.

Offside

Margaret Roach

He toddles towards
his bright new blue and scarlet ball,
kicks it,
finds in surprise
that now his foot
is not at all
conveniently placed
to stand upon,
collapses on the carpet,
bellows annoyance
but rejects with scorn
a helping hand.
He struggles up,
he starts again -
Another footballer has just been born.

Bristol City - the Choice of a New Generation

Andrew Jefferson

I contracted the irreversible football bug at the age of eight after watching West Ham United beat Arsenal 1-0 in the 1980 FA Cup Final. Trevor Brooking scored the only goal on that sunny May afternoon. If you have never heard of Trevor, he is that nice man on the telly who never swears. After the match had finished, I decided to re-enact Brooking's vital goal while my mother attempted to mow the lawn. To me that neatly cut grass was Wembley and between the washing line pole and the fence was the Arsenal goalmouth. Little did Trevor know but he was to score that goal many more times that day. Unfortunately for me the football bug had now bitten.

My father had to crack and eventually after five whole months of my persistent nagging, he finally agreed to take me to my first 'live' football match. Luckily for me he chose to take me to Ashton Gate, home of Bristol City. This late decision would have a profound effect on my life. He could have dragged me kicking and screaming off down to Eastville where I could have joined the ranks of the 'Blue few'. No, the Gods had spoken and fate had determined that I was to become a City supporter.

City were struggling in Division Two at the time after being relegated from the first division the previous season. I was about to watch the first team in English football history to be relegated from the first to the fourth division in consecutive seasons. At least this year we would end up with the small consolation that our near but bitter rivals Bristol Rovers would also join us in the third division. Out opponents that day were Derby County who, like City, had fallen from grace the previous season.

Fifteen years later, I remember very little about that historic first match. It amazes me how some fans can recall almost every detail from their first football experience. Looking back, that Derby County game is a distant memory. I do remember entering the home 'Covered End' from the side of the ground and looking across at the rows of terracing to the massed ranks of the City fans applauding their side. At the time I thought there must have been about 50,000 of them all squashed together like sardines in a tin. I've since learnt that the official crowd attendance that day was 12,020.

It was so packed I had to sit on one of the brightly painted red crush barriers to catch a glimpse of the action on the field. The red paint was just splashed on as if it had been done in a hurry. No workman would have been proud of this job. The actual game was fast and frantic - to a foreigner, a typical British match. I was much more interested, though, in the action on the terraces. Every now and then a shout would go up to be followed by even more sporadic chanting and thousands of people clapping in unison. The atmosphere was electric. Once I thought the roof of the Covered End was going to lift off under the pressure. City's star player at the time was Kevin Mabutt and against Derby he scored two goals to match his status. To this day I still maintain that Mabbsy dedicated those goals to his team's newest supporter. The final score was two each but more importantly I was now a member of the Red army. From now on no football team would ever be deemed worthy enough to take on our beloved City and no visiting supporters would dare have the nerve to try and take the Covered End.

Derby County had a striker playing for them that afternoon called Alan Biley who had long blonde shoulder length hair. He was jeered all afternoon by the City crowd and every now and then chants of "Biley get your hair cut" echoed around the ground. As far as I'm aware Alan Biley still wears his hair shoulder length, so our protests, it seems, were in vain. I never felt settled, sat on that scarlet coloured crash barrier because as soon as there was a surge in the crowd, I would end up falling off. I would jump back on only to fall off again two minutes later as another avalanche of fans came pouring down the terraces. The game seemed to finish before it had even begun. I can still never understand how an hour and a half can pass so quickly. If only Maths lessons could have been like this.

The real fun and games were about to begin once the match had finished. Six thousand people all in a mad rush trying to leave the Covered End in an attempt to get home. I still wonder to this day why people leave football stadiums so early in a blind panic. Are they trying to beat the traffic or are they afraid of missing "Final Score" on the radio? You left the ground through a small exit, the same exit incidentally from where I had entered roughly two hours beforehand. Surely they didn't expect six thousand of us to get through that small gap - but they did and amazingly somehow we all managed it. I lost my dad about three times in the crush and I swear at one stage I felt as if I was being carried along by the sheer weight of the crowd. Thankfully after what seemed an eternity I reached the safety of the car park to live another day. That Trevor Brooking has a lot to answer for.

Captain Marvel and Other Super Heroes

Gordon Dalton

Chips without sauce is like Yorkshire Pudding without gravy is like... Boro without Jamie Pullock. I'm writing this in a cold sweat because even though Jamie has kept faith to Teeside, money is flying around like Noel's House Party.

Jamie is loved by Boro's Barmy Army and any bad tackle, or any tackle for that matter, is greeted by a chant of "Jamie's gona get ya! Jamie's gona get ya!" Despite numerous bad haircuts (goes with the job) Jamie has the hard man image of the team. Although he doesn't look particularly hard, you feel he's just jumped out of the Holygate End and is about to have a go at anyone who takes his fancy. Rather unfairly, he gets booked for trying to return to the terraces to join his mates in celebrating.

If we hadn't been promoted, Jamie would have gone. Even now his place could be in jeopardy - that is, if you believe the back pages of the tabloids. Being exiled in Bristol I only get to see about ten games a year, so I rely heavily on Radio 5 Live, midnight viewings of Endsleigh League Extra (aagghh!) and a daily trudge to the newsagent for information on the best team in the North East. If you think that last bit was biased I don't give a damn, write your own story.

Anyway, now that Captain Marvel himself,

Bryan Robinson, is manager, we get a mention every other day. Unlike the unlucky previous manager, Lennie Lawrence, who wouldn't get a mention in his own programme if he'd eaten the whole squad for his tea.

Mostly it's all transfer speculation, but as the close season drags on we still haven't bought anybody despite having a bid in for everybody. O.K., this could change tomorrow but look at this for a team line up.

Time of going to press: 30/6/95.
Lineker - Match of the day
Papin - Ajax
Baggio - Juventus
Ripley - Blackburn
Helder - Now with Arsenal
Hullit - Now with Chelsea
Gazza - ?
Clarke - Newcastle
Kanchelskis - Manchester Utd
Venison - Now with Galatasery
Collins - Celtic
Unsworth - Q.P.R.
Wright - Liverpool
Hughes - Now Everton

So there's no goalkeeper but let's not split hairs. Boro have had a bid in for all these players.

Personally, I would want all these superheroes at Boro. Mostly of them may be international stars but Middlesbrough is a hard place, as anyone who has passed through the South Bank area won't be able to tell you. They'll be dead or too shocked to speak.

I prefer the players who come under the sub-heading 'crap', 'reliable', 'boring" and 'hard'. Sure, I'd love to have Gazza but these are the players you can shout at. It makes a rainy night at home to Grimsby quite bearable.

Over the years I have had quite a close relationship with this sort of player; and I believe I've had an influential part in their career. You don't believe me? If it's facts you want, it's facts you get.

As a junior Red the then Golden boys of Boro were Stephen Bell and Darren Woods. They would visit our little fan club quite regularly. As any Boro fan will tell you, they weren't so much Golden, just boys; and we treated them as such, taunting them with cruel jibes like, well like only schoolboys can. Our fanclub also sent manager Malcom Allison a lucky duck. The Golden boys sank into obscurity and Allison was sacked.

It is remarkable to think that Alan Kernaghan, now Man City, didn't used to be so bad, well he didn't look bad at Boro. And it is also remarkable to think that he would be playing in our local cricket team one summer. But he did. Alan knew a local butcher and managed to worm his way into our team. He wasn't very good though, in fact he was rather inept. Strange coincidence that. However, he did present me with my best bowler award, and I still show off the photograph without fear of embarrasment. Boro managed to offload him to City for £1.6 million. Suckers.

On a brighter note, my mam recently told me that in the late seventies we nearly bought Stuart Boam's house. Boam was the archetypal

hard man. He nearly looked like he was the love child of Henry Cooper and Bridgitte Nelson (conceived on the North Face of the Eiger). Not that I saw him play or anything important like that. How my mam could have kept this life-changing information from me for so long is beyond me, but that doesn't stop me from telling complete strangers that Boam also drove me round the block in his flash car (probably a maxi).

Talking of cars, I once followed Tony Mowbray in his club car for twenty minutes before losing sight of him. Literally. The next season a Boro favourite was signed by Celtic. Bernie Slaven, strangely another Boro favourite (only because he too liked to climb terrace fencing), was often spotted buying twenty Embassy Regal near the college I was studying at (100 metres from Ayresome Park!). He would scan the local *Evening Gazette* to see if he had been sold. Yes, he had. To Darlington, where upon scoring yet another tap in he tried to scale the fencing only to find there wasn't any. He skulked sheepishly off and embarrassed - for a fag probably.

So now, being promoted and all. I have no intention of meeting Bryan Robinson on Linthorpe Road, I don't want to discuss with John Hendrie why he hasn't been selected for Scotland and I definitely don't want a pint or ten with Jamie Pollock; just in case they all decide to bugger off to higher or lower points (sorry, Alan K.) in their career.

With a new stadium (built with German steel?) and a couple of new players Boro and me can look to day trips to Spurs and Liverpool instead of Southend and Luton. Hopefully we won't be a yo-yo team and go down again. Something nice and mid-table with a good cup run (no third round draws in Wales, please).

After all, we don't want kids up and down the country wearing Boro shirts bearing the legend POLLOCK. Mind you, who'd want to support Middlesbrough F.C?

My Dad thinks...

Anony

Dad doesn't think much of football any more, ever since the World Cup was won in 1966. Football has become boring now and is a namby-pamby game.

...Dad thinks a few more players like Graham Roberts (now manager of Yeovil Town) and Vinny Jones of Wimbledon will make football a lot more exciting.

...My Dad's idea of defence is 15 stud marks up the left nostril. My Dad likes some blood in football. If you don't win with skilful football, be prepared to kick the other team off the pitch.

No Defence

Tony Lewis-Jones

Dribbling a lightweight ball,
My son's left foot
shows promising control.

I encourage skill,
the higher values.
I'm hoping to detect
traces of the genius
that's handed down:

a cousin twice removed,
who wore the red
and knew the voices.

The boy goes past me
and he's quick. My trip,
instinctive, terrible,
cannot be deliberate
though it leaves him
on the floor.

And fifty thousand throats
call 'Off, Off, Off'.

Up the City

Richard Higlett

I started going 'up the City' when I was six years old. I was converted by a promotion for California Raisins, a Royal Marines Brass Band and a 2-0 win over Manchester City. It was the first time I'd caught anything at a match, not the ball or a trombone, but a sample packet of sun dried U.S raisins. Well you know what it's like when you get something unexpected and free, you cherish it, and I did; saving them next to a peanut in a ring box from my uncle's wedding. That day was also the first time I brought the stool that my Dad had 'built'.

It had 1.5" metal tubing legs with industrial rubber feet and was baked in sky blue paint. This was removeable only by nuclear attack. Well it was the 1970s and such things were possible. My dad worked at a factory that made hospital equipment.
Sometimes I'd get hitch-hikers, freeloaders. A difficult to see Tommy Hutchinson corner on the right and tips of strange shoes would invade my blue island. As the ball swung in grown men would cling to me, necks craned, like we were riding the raft from *The Deluge* by Gericault, the painting that hangs in the Tate Gallery. When we scored, my feet left the stool and the whole 'Spion Kop' shimmered and carried me out into a sea of coats and macs, then swung me back to rest on the edge of the stool which instantly flipped and bruised my bony, immature ankles.

I sent it to Gordan Milne for the players to sign but I received a letter apologizing because they could not write, draw, scratch or sandblast into the surface. However, there was a fragment taken from the inside of a leg. I feared that along with photographs, this had been sent to the Pentagon where similar stools were being recreated in Hanger 51 so that extra terrestials could watch all the N.F.L. But Gordon did send me a letter with all the team's autographs, many of whom have now achieved their life time's ambition and own a pub.

After years of faithful service, everyone has got their own seat to stand on, provided by the clubs. My mum still uses the stool to get big pans down or ferret out that elusive bottle of H.P. Fruity from the cupboard's back. It is comforting to know that in its continued use there is still a need and desire to be taller. There is no bruise on my ankle these days but the matches are not quite the same without them.

Football Crazy

M. Markey

"Only having a pineapple for a ball and barefeet meant that playing football could be painful."

The words of a South American Peasant, So poor he couldn't afford food but still chose to kick his weekly free welfare pineapple in his barefeet, until it disintegrated rather than satisfy his hunger.

Foot ball football
Oh how I hate it
Oh it's going on all Night
Tell you I am fed up With it
Boys think it's great
And some of the girls too
Lets hope they put on some more horse riding
Lets hope there Will be less of this football craze.

Illustration and poem by Vicky Harrison